What Works in Grammar Instruction

NCTE Editorial Board

What Works in Grammar Instruction

Deborah Dean
Brigham Young University

NATIONAL COUNCIL OF TEACHERS OF ENGLISH
340 N. NEIL ST., SUITE #104, CHAMPAIGN, ILLINOIS 61820
WWW.NCTE.ORG

Staff Editor: Bonny Graham

Manuscript Editor: The Charlesworth Group

Interior Design: Jenny Jensen Greenleaf

Cover Design: Pat Mayer

Cover Image: iStock.com/Creative-Touch

NCTE Stock Number: 56834; eStock Number: 56841
ISBN 978-0-8141-5683-4; eISBN 978-0-8141-5684-1

It is the policy of NCTE in its journals and other publications to provide a forum for the open discussion of ideas concerning the content and the teaching of English and the language arts. Publicity accorded to any particular point of view does not imply endorsement by the Executive Committee, the Board of Directors, or the membership at large, except in announcements of policy, where such endorsement is clearly specified.

NCTE provides equal employment opportunity to all staff members and applicants for employment without regard to race, color, religion, sex, national origin, age, physical, mental or perceived handicap/disability, sexual orientation including gender identity or expression, ancestry, genetic information, marital status, military status, unfavorable discharge from military service, pregnancy, citizenship status, personal appearance, matriculation or political affiliation, or any other protected status under applicable federal, state, and local laws.

Every effort has been made to provide current URLs and email addresses, but, because of the rapidly changing nature of the web, some sites and addresses may no longer be accessible.

Library of Congress Cataloging-in-Publication Data

Names: Dean, Deborah, 1952- author.

Title: What works in grammar instruction / Deborah Dean.

Description: | Champaign, Illinois : National Council of Teachers of English, 2022. | Includes bibliographical references and index. | Summary: "Addresses the challenges of teaching grammar in the context of reading and writing, providing vignettes of classroom conversations that exemplify what that practice can look like in action"—Provided by publisher.

Identifiers: LCCN 2021049835 (print) | LCCN 2021049836 (ebook) | ISBN 9780814156834 (trade paperback) | ISBN 9780814156841 (adobe pdf)

Subjects: LCSH: English language—Grammar—Study and teaching (Elementary) | English language—Grammar—Study and teaching (Secondary)

Classification: LCC LB1576 .D2827 2022 (print) | LCC LB1576 (ebook) | DDC 372.6/1—dc23/eng/20211116

LC record available at https://lccn.loc.gov/2021049835

LC ebook record available at https://lccn.loc.gov/2021049836

Contents

Preface

When we engage with grammar as art, we allow ourselves to wonder, surrender, be tempted and overcome.

—*Mary Ehrenworth and Vicki Vinton*

"Mrs. Dean?"

I didn't recognize the young man who stopped me next to the giant bags of flour and sugar in Costco. Well, maybe his smile tugged at my memory . . . but, no, I didn't know him.

"You *are* Mrs. Dean, aren't you?

"Yes. I'm sorry . . ."

When he said his name, I remembered. Trevor had been one of two students I had taught all three years of his junior high English. But that had been more than ten years ago and in another state; he'd grown a lot from that slender, shorter-than-average junior high student I had known. He was just finishing college and had gotten married—to an English major, he informed me.

"Are *you* majoring in English?" I asked.

He laughed. Hard. "No way! But, thanks to you, I know grammar better than she does."

I don't know if that was a compliment or not. I had taught Trevor in the beginning of my teaching career, poor guy. In those years, the school district required traditional grammar instruction, despite the fact that publications for the previous decades had endorsed integrating grammar instruction and moving away from traditional approaches. I did what I was expected to do: I taught parts of speech and diagramming, although I modified our text's exercises because I wanted my students to be writers, not grammarians. When the district revised its expectations, asking teachers to teach grammar in context, I was happy to be able to give the time I'd devoted to grammar instruction to writing. But what I found was that I didn't know what "grammar in context" really meant. What was I supposed to do? How was it different?

I know that many of my fellow teachers just dropped grammar altogether. They were happy not to have to teach what they didn't like and what they thought students didn't enjoy. I had liked teaching grammar. I'd had fun—and I think my students had fun, too. We wrote clues for treasure hunts and stories, both consisting of only prepositional phrases, and news stories of absurd events full of adverbs. But teaching grammar in context? That was something I wasn't sure how to do—and no one I talked to seemed to know either.

I read what I could in professional journals and turned to mini-lessons connected to students' writing as my first try. But I think my mini-lessons were a lot like my traditional grammar instruction: using definitions of parts of speech to instruct and then giving students sample sentences from the textbook so they could practice the principles. I just assumed students would transfer such lessons to their writing. When they didn't, I started making more direct connections. That helped some. But I still didn't think this was what it meant to teach grammar in context. Shouldn't it be more integrated with the rest of the course, not just limited to revision days during a writing unit? And how was I to make those mini-lessons more applicable to students' writing?

I've learned a few things since those days. Mostly from trying and revising and trying again. But I've read more and practice more of the ideas I read about in my classes. My teaching didn't change overnight. It evolved—and I think it's still evolving. So now in my position as a teacher educator I think I do a better job when I try to help preservice teachers understand the importance of teaching grammar integrated with the whole language arts. That is, I *think* I do better—until I observe them teach. They tend to teach grammar the way they were taught—either not at all or pretty traditionally. Then I realize that what I've explained doesn't make sense to them. They can't visualize integration. They, too, can't enact "grammar in context."

When I talk with practicing teachers in workshops about integrating grammar into the rest of their course content, I say they should find language in all that their students read and write: "Grammar is all around us." I'm not the first to say it; in *Grammar Alive! A Guide for Teachers* (Haussamen), teachers are told, "You can use the literature the students are reading, as well as newspapers and other texts, to demonstrate or teach almost any grammar lesson" (17). But the practice is harder to implement than that exhortation (or mine) implies. Teachers still look at me, puzzled: "What does it *really* mean?" "What does it *look like* to do that?"

Because of their questions, I have included in this book several snapshots into classroom conversations to show what it can look like to teach grammar in context. The students' names and characters are a composite of students I have taught over the years. The words, obviously, are not actually what students said in one single class. Rather, they are a compilation of classes and comments, very like parts of what happened in several classes. I hope that "seeing" my class in action makes what it means to teach grammar in context more accessible for all teachers.

I hope that my examples show that teaching grammar in context does *not* mean:

- waiting for students to raise language issues
- teaching grammar without any preparation
- teaching grammar only with writing (and only during editing)
- teaching grammar only on Mondays (or Fridays or any other designated day)
- teaching grammar just for a test
- teaching grammar with worksheets

Instead, I hope that my examples show that teaching grammar in context means:

- using grammar as an essential component of meaning-making during reading and writing
- relating language to student experience in a variety of situations
- planning an occasional mini-lesson on a grammar principle
- encouraging regular talk about language as part of class conversation

Chapter 1 sets the stage for teaching an integrated approach to language by briefly exploring the history of grammar instruction and clarifying what we as educators mean when we say we're "teaching grammar." It ends with my explanation of the five aspects of language I use throughout the book to address what I consider to be a comprehensive view of language instruction. Chapter 2 explains what it means to teach language with writing, the most commonly experienced way of integrating grammar. It shows a snapshot into a classroom experience and ends with specific examples that apply to each of the five aspects introduced in the first chapter. Chapter 3 mirrors the previous chapter, except that it deals with integrating language with reading—again ending with specific teaching applications for each of the five aspects. Chapter 4 addresses two major issues that complicate the effective teaching of language for many teachers: concern for English language learners (ELL) and testing. The first part of the chapter explores questions and findings related to these concerns; the chapter ends with specific teaching applications that address these two areas for each of the five aspects of language. Chapters 2, 3, and 4 separate aspects of an integrated approach into discrete topics to make discussion possible; Chapter 5 pulls all the strands back together, exploring how we can implement an integrated approach to language instruction—how we can plan for it and how we can assess it.

There are some other features in this book I should mention. Text boxes labeled "Extending Your Knowledge" accompany the information in the chapters themselves, extending the ideas for readers who want to know more. At the end of each chapter are reflective questions. I hope they provide a way for readers to begin to consider and adapt the ideas for individual classroom needs. In Appendix A, readers will find annotated references that they can use to learn more about the ideas in the different chapters. Appendix B provides some of my personal suggestions about basic grammar knowledge that teachers might consider to begin the language exploration.

Together, I hope these features and the ideas in the chapters themselves will help you as you develop your own classroom dialogues—finding language in all you teach and sharing it with your students.

Author's Note

This is a revision of a book titled *Bringing Grammar to Life*, previously published by the International Reading Association in 2007. This book keeps the same basic shape in terms of titles of chapters and the way the material is divided into those chapters. Mostly that is a function of how classes and lessons work—so it made sense. However, a lot of research and thinking about grammar—in fact, language in general—has occurred in the nearly two decades since I wrote the original manuscript. This new book incorporates that new thinking and research in a variety of ways—in the ways our classroom approaches shift over time and in the ways we see more deeply into grammar issues and their impact on students.

When I wrote the first book, I wanted to address an issue that I (and other teachers who talked to me) experienced as we tried to teach grammar in context: What does it look like? Because that is still an issue, I kept the glimpses into classroom conversations that show how I make those conversations work in classrooms. In the first book, I focused entirely on a novel that used to be taught very regularly, *To Kill a Mockingbird*, and I placed the vignettes at the beginning of each chapter. In this book, I wanted to reflect the wider diversity of texts that are read in classrooms today, so the classroom vignettes now show conversations about a variety of texts.

I have also moved the vignettes around within the chapters so that they make more sense in relation to teaching issues. With regard to the applications that accompany each chapter: some of the ideas previously applied to more traditional texts and types of writing; this new book includes applications that apply to both traditionally taught and more diverse kinds of reading and writing we find in classrooms today. I've also provided a few QR codes in the margin that link to resources for further reading.

Overall, one thing that has not changed is the foundational belief that a teacher's curiosity about and interest in language are essential to making any teaching about grammar work in the classroom—and I hope this heavily revised version still helps teachers see how they can share that interest in their own classrooms.

What Is Grammar?

Grammar is the skunk at the garden party of the language arts.

—*Brock Haussamen*

I collect old grammar books. An odd hobby, I know, but one that helps me get a sense of the history of grammar instruction beyond the summaries I can read in other publications. The preface in one grammar text from 1880 is interesting in how it reveals grammar teaching history and issues. The author, Albert Raub, asserts that "the principles underlying and regulating the use of the English language are best taught by an inductive process" (3). After contrasting his belief with that of what he perceives as the norm—deductive, scientific, and unsuccessful—Raub states that his "design is to teach first the idea, then the name, and lastly the definition" (3). Despite his intent, the book is a series of exercises focused on definitions (that students would have to know before they did the exercises)—nothing so dissimilar from other methods of that time, according to his own description, and certainly not so dissimilar from methods that persisted through most of the next century. Still, it's interesting that, even in 1880, teachers like Raub were aware of the challenges of teaching grammar—and they were proposing solutions not so dissimilar from more recent ones. The book's return in its practices to traditional methods shows how difficult effective instructional methods can be.

Despite pronouncements from the National Council of Teachers of English (NCTE) as early as 1936 and concerns expressed by authors such as Raub, traditional grammar instruction—based on Latin and Greek models and involving memorization of definitions and identification of parts of a sentence—was central to modern education in the United States; that is, it was until the repercussions of *Research in Written Composition* (Braddock et al.) hit. That report contains the following passage, so often repeated as almost to have become a mantra:

In view of the widespread agreement of research studies based upon many types of students and teachers, the conclusion can be stated in strong and unqualified terms: the teaching of formal grammar has a negligible or, because it usually displaces some instruction and practice in actual composition, even a harmful effect on the improvement of writing. (37–38)

Braddock and colleagues' report started a controversy that was argued in journals for the next two decades. In fact, in 1985, Hartwell made the observation that both sides argued from the same research but that "prior assumptions about the value of teaching grammar" colored the interpretation of that research (106): people saw what they wanted to see. Hillocks's 1986 findings, more than twenty years after the Braddock report, reinforced the earlier findings and contributed to spreading its perspective: "The study of traditional school grammar . . . has no effect on raising the quality of student writing. . . . Taught in certain ways, grammar and mechanics instruction has a deleterious effect on student writing" (248). Since the mid-1980s, this conclusion has largely been accepted as the final word in the controversy: teaching grammar in traditional ways does nothing to improve writing.

Hartwell's assertion about how teachers interpret research findings depending on their prior assumptions certainly seems apparent in the way teachers responded to the reports from Braddock and his colleagues and, later, Hillocks. Some teachers saw the reports as an excuse to throw out grammar instruction: at last, they could stop doing what they hated and what their students seemed to hate. Some teachers believed that, if grammar instruction didn't help students develop as writers, there was no value in teaching it. Others didn't want to give the impression that students' home languages weren't of value. For whatever reason, in many classes, students received no grammar instruction.

Teachers holding a grammarian perspective, believing in the effects of traditional grammar instruction despite the reports' findings, continued to teach grammar. Battistella suggests that along with this persistent belief in the academic value of teaching traditional grammar was a moral element, a feeling that good grammar was somehow reflective of good character and therefore ought to be taught. Teachers who persisted in teaching traditional grammar, though, were often seen as out of step with current theory and practice, so they withdrew from local discussions and sometimes hid what they taught in the classroom. According to Wallace, they were "driven underground" (2).

One (possibly unintended) consequence of the pronouncements from Braddock and colleagues and Hillocks is that grammar was linked almost solely with writing instruction. Both reports state that traditional grammar instruction does not improve students' *writing*—thus effectively limiting any other application for language instruction. What developed from this narrowed perspective is an approach toward grammar instruction called "teaching grammar in context," which is a response to an emphasis on the writing process and was popularized in the well-known book of the same name (Weaver). Lobeck comments on the consequence of this limited view of grammar's value: "The popular idea of teaching grammar only 'in context' perpetuates a narrow view of the applications of grammatical knowledge to other areas of study in the K–12 curriculum" (100). Grammar as helpful to reading, grammar as related to language attitudes, or grammar as anything other than punctuation and correction seemed to be ignored in the rush to contextualize grammar as part of writing process instruction.

With the new focus on grammar for writing, some teachers tried to do what seemed to be the logical outcome of the research—they tried to integrate grammar into writing instruction. But many teachers found this stance problematic in a number of ways. Because integrated grammar instruction necessitates individual application, there is little that can be given to teachers to use in class in the way of texts or planned lessons. Teachers have to develop mini-lessons that respond to students' needs. As a consequence, teachers need something that's in short supply in public schools: time. They need time to analyze students' needs and time to prepare materials that will help meet those needs.

As a result, I see teachers resort to such strategies as daily oral and written practice using sentences from a textbook or website that students correct as a class. These sentences generally contain a range of errors, from a lack of punctuation at the end of a sentence to the use of commas in restrictive and nonrestrictive clauses. If a student is having trouble with sentence boundaries, I can't imagine that they would be ready to learn about the complexities of which clause is essential and which is not. Furthermore, the sentences reduce grammar to a hunt for errors—and in sentences that aren't even the students' own! How do they understand what the writer intended to communicate? In most classes I observe, teachers make no application beyond correcting the sentences with the students—and then consider their teaching of language—grammar—done! Dust off my hands.

Time isn't made any easier when researchers like Myhill et al. find that effective grammar instruction requires lots of talk:

Through this kind of exploratory talk, students are given ownership in making writerly decisions and are enabled to "make informed judgements about language," questioning rather than compliantly accepting "socially defined notions of 'good grammar.'" (107, citing Denham and Lobeck)

This talk about language takes time—another drain on what teachers have in little supply. But it has another complicating factor: it also requires a certain level of language knowledge on the teacher's part. And many teachers I speak with find this almost threatening. What if they don't know what the students are asking about? What if they don't know how to explain the language constructions they are reading and writing?

And new textbooks aren't always helpful either. An analysis of popular writing texts commonly found in schools shows that they include significantly more about writing than previous versions and that those sections are moved to the front of the texts, emphasizing writing. These texts include some grammar lessons in the writing chapters, in addition to the traditional grammar section that has been moved to the back of the book. Despite the appearance of integration of grammar instruction with writing, these texts "miss what is essential in real integration: connection with the concerns that are actually occurring in students' writing" (Dean, "Underground" 31). Instead, the texts include a lesson on pronoun agreement with descriptive writing, for example, even though pronoun agreement may not be what is needed for students who are writing descriptions. The texts give the appearance of integration in what is really an almost impossible task for a text, because integration relies on the teacher's recognition of individual students' needs with specific pieces of writing or reading. For some teachers, all these challenges are just too much. The result? "The 'right moment' hardly ever arose and grammar was simply not taught at all" (Hudson 102).

The teaching of grammar has an interesting past, a complicated intertwining of conflicting goals and purposes. The issues of what research shows and what teachers should do about research findings seem to be—at least to some extent—resolved. In a 2001 themed issue of *Voices from the Middle*, the editor summarized the thinking of the time: "The question isn't 'Do we teach grammar?' but instead 'How do we teach grammar in context?'" (Beers 4). In the decades since, we have been trying to answer the question. Part of the answer might be in how we define the term: what does *grammar* mean?

Well, that depends on whom we ask.

Hartwell, in refining Francis's classic "three meanings of grammar," provides five meanings for the term:

1. *Grammar 1*—the patterns of language people all learn intuitively as they learn a language. Hartwell calls this the "grammar in our head" and describes its "internalized" and "abstract" nature, as well as its connection to "the acquisition of literacy" (111). He gives an example to show Grammar

1 by listing a series of words and noting how native speakers always know the way to order the words to achieve meaning.

2. *Grammar 2*—the scientific aspect of language that analyzes and studies patterns of language. This grammar, Hartwell (and others) argues, is not of much value in schools because it is more concerned with theoretical factors than reality.

3. *Grammar 3*—what Francis termed "linguistic etiquette" (Hartwell 109) and what Hartwell calls "usage." Grammar 3 deals with issues of language that may have social consequences. If a person breaks the rules of Grammar 3, they may be thought uneducated, probably unworthy, and, possibly, immoral.

4. *Grammar 4*—school grammar. Although scientific grammar and school grammar are linked, Hartwell calls Grammar 4 unscientific because of its "inadequate principle": a concern with logic and a false connection to Latin (110). In his further discussions of Grammar 4, he refers to the rules teachers teach about language as "incantations." He argues that these rules make sense only if a person already understands the concept—that the rules themselves cannot teach the concepts—and he provides examples of possessives and fragments to make his point.

5. *Grammar 5*—"stylistic grammar" or grammar as it relates to teaching writing, particularly at the sentence level (111). Today, Grammar 5 might even be broader and considered as *rhetorical grammar*, which moves beyond the sentence level in most cases. Hartwell anticipated this move somewhat by noting that "writers need to develop skill at two levels. One, broadly rhetorical, involves communication in meaningful contexts. The other, broadly metalinguistic rather than linguistic, involves active manipulation of language with conscious attention to surface form" (125). Today, references to grammar as style might refer to either level.

Since Hartwell's article, others have presented alternate definitions of grammar in an attempt to ensure that, when teachers talk about what we are teaching, we are talking about the same thing—and not simply focusing on issues of correctness. The definition in *Grammar Alive! A Guide for Teachers* (Haussamen) condenses Hartwell's five meanings into two, essentially Grammar 1 and Grammar 5. Although this categorization is simpler, it doesn't address oral use of language in formal situations. Burke, citing Kress and van Leeuwen, provides an even broader definition: grammar as "patterns of experience, enabl[ing] human beings to build a mental picture of reality, to make sense of their experience of what goes on around them and inside them" ("Developing" 60). And Crovitz and Devereaux would agree: "Crazy as it may sound, grammar is really about understanding, not about 'correctness'" (*Grammar* 2). So. We have lots of voices trying to establish what we mean when we say *grammar*.

For the purposes of this book, I use *grammar* and *language* interchangeably, but my use is intended to embrace several of the perspectives I've presented here: grammar involves learning about language from a variety of perspectives to help students read, write, and speak in meaningful ways in a variety of contexts.

Why Should We Teach Grammar?

Weaver (*Teaching Grammar* 3–6) cites several reasons often given for teaching grammar, including the following:

- to train the brain
- to aid in learning a second language
- to help students score well on large-scale tests
- to help them speak in socially prestigious ways
- to help them improve as writers and readers

After she discounts these reasons as invalid or ineffective because of research findings, she still suggests teaching grammar as a means of improving writing. Her recommendation to eliminate traditional grammar instruction in order to allow more time for writing seems to address the conflicting issues raised in research. This highly endorsed perspective—that we limit the focus of instruction to a few concepts and that we teach grammar primarily to improve writing—is dominant in published literature on grammar instruction.

However, other educators and researchers make different arguments for studying language. Penha says we don't need a reason, that "by definition" that is what we do as English teachers (20). Donna echoes this point when she compares goals for studying history or math with those of teaching language: "In stark contrast to other disciplines, the formal study of language in our schools too often ignores these four goals, doing little to establish basics, inspire wonder, train useful skills, or support advanced study" (67). Her point makes a good case for incorporating language study into other aspects of a language arts course: to expose students to ideas about language and to generate interest in its issues. When I've approached grammar this way—as a way to inspire curiosity and interest in language—my experience has been that students are fascinated to learn more about something that is so integral to their daily lives. Noden's response to the question of why teach grammar is poetic:

> I teach grammar because it is the doorway to the human soul.
>   Its intricacies trigger our laughter, our tears, our dreams. Grammar is the secret muse of all expression, the portrait painter of life's emotions.…Nothing in life is more essential, more sensitive, more intrinsic to the human soul.…How could we not teach grammar? (19)

I have to echo Noden: "How could we not?"

What Aspects of Grammar Should We Teach?

Many educators ask this question—and lots of educators try to answer it. Some of the answer depends on the purpose: if we teach grammar for writing, we might teach different things than if we are teaching it for academic purposes (testing) or for reading. Whatever we teach, grammar gurus like Constance Weaver (e.g., in "Teaching Grammar in the Context of Writing") and Harry Noden suggest that we use only minimum terminology and don't expect students to memorize definitions. In fact, Noden often uses descriptors to help students navigate grammar; for example, identifying a *participle* as "an *ing* verb tagged on the beginning or end of a sentence" (4). For me, this advice opens up a world of possibility, teaching grammar in ways that students can make their own and that can be meaningful for their purposes.

I will admit to the challenges of this approach. Once, I was teaching a writing class for students who had failed other English classes. After looking at several examples, students defined an *appositive* as a group of words that comes after a noun and says it another way. In Justine's writing log, where she was expected to identify strategies authors used to enhance their writing, she annotated a sentence from her reading with this comment: "Its an example of a positive [*sic*]." I read her sentence several times wondering "a positive *what*?" I finally asked my husband to listen as I read her sentence aloud, assuming he might help me figure out the meaning. As soon as I read the words aloud, her meaning was clear. She was identifying appositives in her reading; because I had only named the structure and hadn't stressed the spelling, she was doing the best she could. She could identify and use appositives—but she couldn't spell or define them. That's one possible consequence of this approach, one not entirely negative. Just something to be aware of.

If we look at the International Reading Association (IRA)/NCTE standards (particularly 4, 6, 9, and 12), we could say that we should teach language (grammar) for both oral and written communication and we should teach students that the use of language varies depending on the context and purpose for that communication—moving beyond simply oral and written styles to involve genre and audience considerations. Students should know something about language, its structure and conventions, so that they can use that knowledge to help them read and interpret language in a variety of texts. Students should learn about language diversity—and the history of the language as well as something about language change that is inherent in that knowledge—so that they might become respectful of variety in language use.

By considering these standards and the suggestions of knowledgeable voices in the field, I have developed my own list of what we should teach. I recognize that any list I develop will not address everything. I am guided by a sense of language and grammar as more than just an influence on writing; I see it as an aspect of living, both in and out of the classroom. I'm certain that readers may want to add or delete some items. However, in looking at traditional concerns as well as linguistic concerns with language, in thinking about what we hope to achieve with language instruction in the classroom, and in considering what a language arts teacher could feasibly learn and address, I feel these areas are the most encompassing and pertinent. All are meant to be addressed in the context of the other activities in the classroom, not just with writing:

- traditional grammar
- editing
- usage
- language change
- rhetorical grammar

Traditional Grammar

Before anyone closes the book at this first item, I need to differentiate what I mean by this term from what is normally called *traditional grammar*, which is known for worksheets, memorizing definitions, diagramming, and so forth—all separated from anything else in the curriculum. There are many reasons to avoid teaching traditional school grammar (what Hartwell labeled as Grammar 4). Haussamen notes an important one: "Instead of helping students to focus on real literature or on the actual paper they are writing, traditional grammar pedagogy requires students to divert their attention to the isolated and often contrived sentences in a textbook" (xiii). Even more fundamental, however, is the fact that traditional grammar instruction involves defining terms—and the definitions don't really work.

Schuster makes the same point central to his book *Breaking the Rules: Liberating Writers through Innovative Grammar Instruction*:

> The thesis of this book is that traditional school grammar has left a heritage of definitions that do not define and rules that do not rule (in usage, writing, and punctuation). These inadequate definitions and mythrules hamper students rather than help them in their development as speakers and writers. (191)

He provides multiple examples in case anyone reading this book isn't convinced. And our own experiences as teachers should add weight to these claims. I can't say how many times I've been frustrated or have frustrated students who don't understand some aspect of grammar by using a definition to help them learn. My experience supports Hillocks and Smith's assertion: "Traditional school grammar presents definitions that cannot function with desired results unless the person using them has more information about language than the definition provides" (723). That is certainly the case when I have tried to teach sentence boundaries to some students by using only the traditional "definition" of a sentence.

So, if we are all clear on the negative aspects of traditional grammar, why do I include it here? I do so primarily for the sake of concept and vocabulary. Students need to know the concepts of sentences and parts of speech. Respected writers on the subject, including Weaver, Noguchi (*Grammar*), and Noden, use grammatical terms such as *adjectives, subjects, verbs, clauses,* and *phrases* when they discuss language and writing. And, in Chapter 8 of *Grammar Alive! A Guide for Teachers* (Haussamen), which provides a great overview of linguistic grammar, some traditional terms are used along with other terms. Some words just are necessary for instruction, and the traditional terms are more universal. I am not saying we should teach these terms by definition and ask students to memorize them and identify them in sentences for a test (unless you have to practice that for state testing—but that's in another chapter) or that students should know the parts of a sentence so that they can diagram them in exercises from textbooks. But being able to generalize about the terms we use so that students can connect them to their innate knowledge of language concepts and use them to improve their abilities with activities that involve language (reading, writing, speaking) is important for the other things students do in classes.

Going back to Grammar 1, I think students develop very early a sense of parts of speech. In other words, they sense that certain words name things and other words explain what those things do and other words describe either the thing or the action. Most students possess this kind of sense about words, and it's evident even when we hear toddlers speaking that they comprehend the idea of how words function. What I'm suggesting is that we use that Grammar 1 knowledge as a foundation for a common vocabulary that will allow us to talk about language in the classroom. In the same way Noden describes an appositive as a "noun that adds a second image to a preceding noun" (7), we can use a few basic terms from traditional grammar to aid us in language discussions with students. I want to make clear that I am not advocating diagramming sentences (although I personally like the challenge of it) or memorizing definitions or testing students' ability to identify parts of speech in sentences in textbooks. What I am advocating is that some of the terms—for want of anything better—can be useful to us as we talk to students about language and what it does.

And I don't think we have to rely only on the traditional definitions when we talk about the few terms we want to use. Because they don't work completely anyway and because students often have a sense of what the concepts are, let them help define the terms. Even if they don't get a definition that will explain every instance, the generalization will stick with them. If I want to talk about the verbs in a text or in my students' writing, I can have students decide what verbs are and what they do from students' own experience and from investigation of the texts in front of us—not to identify every verb (a traditional grammar kind of thing to do) but to discover how verbs make the author's intent clear or make the text more inviting to read. Then we could discuss how these ideas about verbs could be helpful to them as writers.

Other educators have written their suggestions for additional ways to explore some of the traditional aspects of grammar that teachers need to address without relying on the traditional definitions that don't work. Noguchi offers suggestions for finding the subject of a sentence through questioning ("Rethinking"). Schuster recommends several ideas for investigating parts of speech, including test frames for prepositions and an activity that helps students understand the differing effects of coordinating and conjunctive conjunctions. Using terms from traditional grammar does not mean a return to memorization of definitions or worksheets or diagramming. We can talk about language with traditional terms, as needed, but teach them and use them in much more varied ways that have application to the rest of the work we do with students in our classes.

Editing

I remember my brother-in-law telling me about a job he'd interviewed for. The interviewer told him that more than two hundred applicants had applied for that one position. The first cut was made on the basis of editing: if an application had a punctuation or grammatical error, it was tossed. Because this was an engineering job, I was surprised. I guess I thought those things mattered mostly to English teachers—at least that's what I hear all the time.

Writers haven't always been concerned with punctuation. It wasn't necessary in earliest written texts (at least in Western civilization) because the texts were read aloud anyway. Scribes who wrote the speeches were mostly concerned with accurately representing the words of the speaker. In fact, the words were written without breaks between them, let alone markings to indicate any other pause. But, according to Parkes, since the sixth century, when reading silently started to be more of an expectation, conventions to aid the reader were developed and refined to address the changing needs of readers over time.

At first, since most of the texts were religious, scribes and monks were concerned that the markings to help readers should support orthodox interpretations (Parkes), showing even very early that writers understood how punctuation could affect meaning. Early punctuation marks were not standardized; the size was often in relation to previous words or letters, and changes occurred in what the punctuation represented over time. One example I find interesting is the use of the ivy leaf. In the 800s, it was only a printer's ornament. So it went from being functional to simply decorative. I'm sure some of our students wish commas or apostrophes would make the same switch.

From the twelfth century on, we are more likely to see punctuation similar to today's, and we can thank Irish and Anglo-Saxon scribes because they developed many of today's conventions as they worked with Latin (another language) and tried to create smaller texts. Even with similar marks, however, Schuster notes that "punctuation conventions are always in flux" (*Breaking* 151), and anyone who reads emails knows that is true. Schuster, in an analysis of a grammar book from 1762, notes that at that time "writers typically used about three times more punctuation than we do today" (151). Our students should be happy to know that fewer marks mean fewer chances for error.

Despite the popularity of Truss's book *Eats, Shoots and Leaves: The Zero Tolerance Approach to Punctuation* and a sense that differing attitudes about punctuation are only modern, feelings about what punctuation should do for writers go back to attitudes and philosophies of the seventeenth and eighteenth centuries. At that time, John Locke's philosophy, represented in the view that language "ought to be subjected to a process of careful regulation with a view to achieving correctness and precision for the expression and communication of ideas" (qtd. in Parkes 91), countered a rhetorical view (supported by elocutionists like Thomas Sheridan) that written language should be more like speech, that punctuation should help reflect the speaker's emphasis and inclinations. That argument is still one we see today—the conflict between strict adherence to rules and a kind of flexibility that allows writers to shape meaning through punctuation marks.

Thinking about how punctuation can shape meaning reminds me of a note my grandson brought home from school. It was from his second-grade teacher. My daughter-in-law sent me a picture of it (see Figure 1.1) and asked me how she was meant to interpret it. The question of interpretation is all caused by punctuation. Is her son truly interesting? Or is the teacher suggesting some

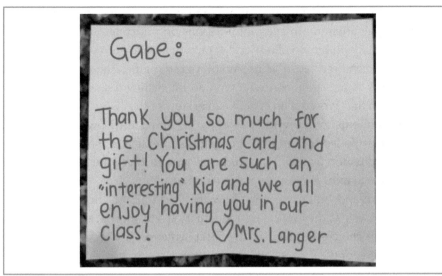

FIGURE 1.1. Teacher note uses "interesting" punctuation.

alternative way to understand how she sees Gabe? Is he interesting in a way that the teacher doesn't appreciate? I don't know, but the teacher's use of a simple punctuation mark caused a lot of consternation in the family. Punctuation matters.

By the term *editing*, I mean gaining an understanding of the use of punctuation not only for correctness but also for meaning-making and style. I have taught punctuation both ways, and, although knowing the "rules" is sometimes useful, I really believe it isn't as effective as learning punctuation by paying attention to how it affects meaning in texts—our own and others':

> With your comma here, I group these ideas together and separate them from this
> idea. Is that what you want me to do?

But students also need to have a sense of how others read punctuation—the rules—so that they can interpret texts effectively. Just as drivers "read" a red light as a signal to stop, readers know from the "rules" what different forms of punctuation signal. It's a balancing act, to know how much "rule" and how much "sense" we should teach. Ehrenworth and Vinton describe the tension well: students "need to own the rules and grammar, not be enslaved to them" (88). How to accomplish both tasks is the hard part.

One way to accomplish the balance is recommended by Atwell, among others: *mini-lessons*, which are short, teacher-directed lessons focused on a specific topic related to students' current writing. In responding to the concern that students don't pay attention to even mini-lessons on punctuation, Atwell asserts (and I agree) that "students will respond to punctuation lessons when the content is relevant—when they need the information to strengthen their writing" (238). She introduces punctuation concerns with an interesting lesson on the history of punctuation that provides an effective overview of the "why" of punctuation and allows students to apply the lesson by inventing their own punctuation. I've tried the same lesson and find it engages students and makes them more aware of punctuation as a way to guide readers; furthermore, it makes them more receptive to mini-lessons on punctuation.

Ehrenworth and Vinton describe how they read aloud—not only to show intonation but also as they reflect the punctuation—to show students the effect of punctuation choices in texts. They collect sentences and texts that provide strong examples for the discussions they have in class to showcase the punctuation they are learning. As they describe it:

> To get students to engage in grammar this way, we need to make it seductive, something they can't resist. We need to make them want to play with it, to dig in and get their hands dirty. We need to stop imposing it on them and invite them to explore it with us, discovering for themselves why the rules are there and what meaningful purpose they serve. (89)

Editing is an important skill for students to learn. As teachers, we can help them learn through their writing, but we don't always need to wait until students are ready to polish a piece of writing to address editing concerns. We can address issues related to punctuation in our reading and in our talking, too. We can find examples for teaching punctuation all around us—in advertisements, in music, in memes and tweets. When students become sensitive to this aspect of language, they gain immeasurably in preparation for their lives outside of school as well as in their reading and writing.

Usage

We're all aware that usage is the aspect of grammar most people expect us to teach and to monitor. When strangers find out we're English teachers, they often respond, "I'd better watch my grammar around you." They don't mean their punctuation; they mean their usage. Usage issues evoke deep emotions about language. Out of respect for students' home languages, some teachers avoid addressing issues of usage, considering that what is taught under the category of usage demeans the home language and perpetuates the power inherent in standardized forms of English.

But Ehrenworth and Vinton make a strong case for the opposite approach: "Teaching students the language of power does not necessarily mean asking them to conform to it. It means giving them the knowledge they will need to make informed and meaningful language choices" (6). In fact, they note that ignoring the issues of power inherent in language usage actually works against students' agency: "We hearken to Delpit's plea that 'to act as if power does not exist is to ensure that the power status quo remains the same'" (52).

As teachers, we can (and should) help students understand Standard English more from a position of what it is (regularized) and what it is not (inherently better). Wikipedia made this distinction clear in its definition of *Standard English* (this entry has been revised since I accessed it):

> In an English-speaking country, Standard English (SE) is the variety of English that has undergone substantial regularization and is associated with formal schooling, language assessment, and official print publications, such as public service announcements and newspapers of record, etc. The term "Standard" refers to the regularization of the grammar, spelling, usages of the language, and not to minimal desirability or interchangeability (e.g., a standard measure). There are substantial differences among the language varieties that countries of the Anglosphere identify as "standard English." . . . Sociologically, as the standard language of the nation, Standard English is generally associated with education and sociolinguistic prestige, but is not inherently superior to other dialects of English used by an Anglophone society. [*sic*]

As the Wikipedia article notes, even in different English-speaking countries, there are a variety of Englishes. Wheeler and Swords, referring to *The Stories of English* (Crystal), identify "nearly sixty popular varieties of international Standard Englishes" (127). And Birch notes that there are at least four "standard dialects within Standard American English," including variations between spoken and written forms (4–5).

All of this strengthens the point that Joseph Williams makes: "We must reject the notion that observing the rules of Standard English makes anyone intellectually or morally superior. That belief is not just factually wrong; in a socially diverse democracy, it is destructive" (14). But it is not an uncommon belief—in schools and outside of them, too. Once, I wrote a thank-you note to a neighbor and gave it to him with a plate of cookies. Later, I was stunned when he expressed his surprise that as an English teacher I would have used a double negative in my note. I was surprised that as a magazine editor he couldn't see that I had used it to create an effect. But I learned a lesson about Standard English: audience matters even when the genre is informal. With even a limited exposure to these ideas, students can understand that the concepts related to usage are crucial for them as readers, speakers, and writers. Raising their awareness of these issues can help them make good choices in their own use of language, as well as become more flexible in their judgments about others' usage.

Tightly connected to usage issues is an understanding of language variety in all its forms: dialects, levels of formality, cultural differences. At the very least, teachers need to help students realize that language varies among people, among situations, and for different purposes. Even more, we should help students come to understand and appreciate this variety. I appreciate Schuster's introduction to dialects: "I speak a dialect, you speak a dialect, all God's children speak dialects, because, as linguist John McWhorter ["Power"] says, dialects are all there is/are/be" (*Breaking* 62). Schuster then relates a personal story of his own acquisition of standard dialect while retaining—and using it when effective—the dialect he learned growing up. Dialects, especially those that are not considered standard, arouse responses in listeners. We attach judgments because of those responses. Jamila Lyiscott's "3 Ways to Speak English" TED Talk about her dialects might be a good way to help students begin to consider attitudes toward dialects.

I will never forget what I learned as a new college student. I attended a talk by a guest lecturer who was to speak about his book on the origins of colloquial phrases. After a faculty member gave a laudatory introduction, the lecturer began to speak, but not in the dialect of academia I had expected. He used a rural Appalachian dialect instead. In the first place, I had trouble understanding some of what he said; in the second, the thought came into my mind wondering what he had to say that could be of value to me. I guess I had forgotten the credentials mentioned in the introduction and my own professed acceptance of dialects. Suddenly, he switched dialects and began speaking in the one I expected for the situation. In shock, I realized the trap I had fallen into, judging him based on his dialect. While we know it is unacceptable to discriminate on so many aspects of our individuality—race, gender, sexuality, and so on—we often still discriminate on the basis of language. Attitudes about language use, especially negative ones, persist.

Recognizing what dialects are is a start to moving past language discrimination. Students should understand that dialects have grammar, that they follow rules, and that they are simply a variety of language. Wheeler and Swords explain that "since any language variety is like a fully stocked kitchen, any dialect

. . . has the wherewithal to express whatever speakers need" (13). In other areas of their lives outside of school, students appreciate variety and self-expression. Just ask them about the issue of wearing uniforms to school! Students always bring up self-expression as a primary reason against any policy that regulates their clothing. In a similar way, students can come to appreciate and understand the benefits that language diversity can add to their own lives as well as to the world. I overheard a ninth grader's comment to a friend: "I speak three languages: Utah, Pig Latin, and English." He, obviously, was aware that he used language differently in different situations. When students realize that they are multidialectal, they should consider how certain audiences might respond to some of their dialects as a way to begin thinking about attitudes toward dialects.

Another way students can come to appreciate a variety of dialects is through literature. Many of the novels and short stories students read in school show characters who speak in dialects; these pieces of literature allow us to address issues of language variety with our students as they explore the richness of language available to all of us through dialects. When we consider the characters, their lives, and their uses of language, we can begin to consider, too, our own lives and language—and our attitudes about them.

Although some teachers use an approach to usage and dialect instruction called *code-switching*, more recent thinking about this issue finds that code-switching, even inadvertently, may actually still encourage the belief that one dialect is better than another, may still silence some of the voices in our classrooms. More current thinking suggests, instead, encouraging *code-meshing*. Code-meshing involves blending dialects more than switching between/among them. Barret explains the advantage of code-meshing as follows: "By extending the range of grammatical forms that students may use to express themselves, code-meshing recognize[s] the importance of *both* Standard and undervalued varieties in contexts beyond the classroom" (Young et al. 43). In many places, both print and public, we can see examples of code-meshing that can help students begin to see how it works to communicate in the world.

In fact, code-meshing isn't really new. As Young et al. acknowledge:

> Contrary to popular beliefs about the so-called proper way that we should write and speak, few people, if any, exclusively adhere to the narrow rules of Standard English when communicating, even in professional, public, or formal settings. Really, most people are more profoundly affected by and interested in prose that brings together colorful language, local idioms, cultural vernaculars, the grammars of various ethnic groups, and now more than ever, techno-lingo—all of which represents code-meshing. (77)

Young and colleagues encourage teachers to ask students to consider their own uses of language and the language of others as a way to begin to notice how we are all shaped by and communicate with language unique to our lives; they also encourage teachers to help students see how often people use code-meshing in social media such as Twitter, but also in news articles, books, and other print texts. Seeing how usage is fluid and much more than a duality—Standard and something else—can help all of our students find their voices in our classrooms and in the world, can help them consider the myriad ways they might use their language resources to communicate effectively.

Language Change

I find Winchester's description of the changeable nature of English very compelling:

> And though George Orwell might have longed for an Anglo-Saxon revival, though John Dryden loathed French loanwords, despite Joseph Addison's campaigns against contractions such as *mayn't* and *won't*, and although Alexander Pope pleaded for retention of dignity and Daniel Defoe wrote of his hatred of the "inundation" of curse-words and Jonathan Swift mounted a life-long attempt to "fix our language forever"—no critic and advocate of immutability has ever once managed properly or even marginally to outwit the English language's capacity for foxy and relentlessly slippery flexibility.
>
> For English is a language that simply cannot be fixed, nor can its use ever be absolutely laid down. It changes constantly; it grows with an almost exponential joy. It evolves eternally; its words alter their senses and their meanings subtly, slowly, or speedily according to fashion and need. (29)

Even though students might find that first sentence challenging to understand—and may not understand the implications of the names Winchester lists—the sense of how many people have sought to stop changes to English should be clear. Understanding the changeable nature of language helps students make

John McWhorter explains how many of us think that language change is appropriate when we bring in new words for new ideas but may not be as happy about other kinds of language change. However, change is what language does:

> Rather marvelous, then, is that precisely the kinds of things that sound so disorderly, so inattendant, so "wrong," are precisely how Latin became French. The way people under a certain age use *totally* and the pronunciation of *nuclear* as "nucular" are not some alternate kind of language change sitting alongside the "real" kind. Language change like this is all there has ever been. (*Words* 3)

the transition to understanding language variation. In differentiating between change and variation, Denham says the old maxim of "majority rules" is the best judge: "When a substantial number of speakers have adopted the variation as their own accepted pronunciation or grammatical form, then we say that the language has changed" (150). To develop awareness of language change, students could identify words that are currently finding their way into the English language—or teachers could introduce them to the idea of language change by telling them which words have been adopted for dictionaries each year.

Change is a fascinating aspect of language, so, in addressing language change, it's important for students to realize that change isn't a bad thing, that it doesn't mean that language is getting worse. Instead, it is an important indicator that language is alive and meeting the needs of its users. As an example, in the preface to the 1937 grammar book *An A.B.C. of English Usage*, Canby makes this observation after lamenting the inevitable acceptance of *contact* as a verb (as in *I contacted him*): "Nothing is more characteristic of the peculiar genius of English than the ease with which it has always expanded by using nouns as verbs, verbs as adjectives, and more rarely adjectives as nouns" (7). In Figure 1.2, Calvin addresses just such shifting. His comments can help students consider their own expansions of language: Have they adopted or created any new words in the last year? Have they moved a word from its traditional usage to a new one? Shakespeare was a master at such expansion, and students can be directed to some of the ways his innovative use of language contributed to how we use language today. Comparing words older people use to those students now use can provide useful insights on helping students recognize that language change does not diminish the language.

Denham addresses language death with her students, noting that scholars predict that "in this century, as many as 95 percent of the estimated 6,000 languages currently spoken in the world may become extinct" (154). This indicates the highest language death rate ever. Students might not care, thinking that their language isn't dying. But helping them consider how identity and language are

FIGURE 1.2. Calvin and Hobbes cartoon: Verbing. (CALVIN AND HOBBES © 1993 Watterson. Reprinted with permission of ANDREWS MCMEEL SYNDICATION. All rights reserved.)

closely tied can help them understand their own language better as well as have concern for other languages. Raised in Alaska, I'd heard that the Natives had many more words for *snow* than we did; Bryson confirms it: "Fifty words . . . crunchy snow, soft snow, fresh snow, and old snow, but no word that just means snow" (14). Bryson also gives examples of words that other languages have that English doesn't, concluding that these words reveal something about the cultures that developed them. Helping students see how language is connected to identity by finding ways that their own language reflects their identity can help them appreciate language death as well as language change.

Even a brief introduction to the history of English can help students gain understanding about language change. A number of books—and a very interesting documentary series—on the history of English are available (see Figure 1.3 for some examples). Atwell has a good "brief history of the English language"

Extending Your Knowledge

In the introduction to her book *Lost in Translation*, Ella Sanders explains her interest in words that are found in some languages but not translated into others. Possibly because they represent an idea unique to the culture associated with the language?

> Language wraps its understanding and punctuation around us all, tempting us to cross boundaries and helping us to comprehend the impossibly difficult questions that life relentlessly throws at us. ("Introduction")

Among the words she lists in the book are these two that I find fascinating:

Gurfa (Arabic)—"the amount of water that can be held in a hand"
Komorebi (Japanese)—"the sunlight that filters through the leaves of trees"

These words, and others in the book, encourage me to be more curious about finding words for concepts that we might not have a word for. That is something I wish for students, too.

Bragg, Melvin. *The Adventure of English: The Biography of a Language.* Arcade, 2011.[a]
Bryson, Bill. *The Mother Tongue: English and How It Got That Way.* William Morrow, 1990.
Crystal, David. *The Cambridge Edition of the History of the English Language.* 3rd ed., Cambridge UP, 2019.
"The Story of English." Directed by William Cran, *Documentaries Plus*, 21 Sep. 2010, documentaries -plus.blogspot.com/2010/09/story-of-english.html.
[a]This is a companion book to a British television series of the same name, presented by Bragg, first broadcast in November 2003 (*The Adventure of English*).

FIGURE 1.3. Sample titles that can provide background on the history of English.

that she uses in a mini-lesson (209–12). Bryson's book *The Mother Tongue* has a fascinating first chapter that provides great examples about English as a way to engage students' interest in their language. He provides examples for the aspects of English that set it apart: the richness of vocabulary, its flexibility, its conciseness, (arguably) its ease of spelling and pronunciation. He says its most notable trait, however, is "its deceptive complexity" (19). All of these aspects relate in some way to the history of the language; I know from experience that even a little background on that history can help students understand aspects of language that they might otherwise find confusing or miss altogether.

One aspect of language change that has immediacy for students is related to spelling and irregular verbs. An understanding of the history of English with its influences from other language can help students see why some words don't follow the spelling rules we learn in elementary school.

- Irregular plurals are left over from Old English patterns (e.g., *oxen*, *mice*, *geese*), words that haven't yet followed the tendency to regularize that other words did (Denham).

- Other spelling irregularities also derive from historical events. Because scribes originally used the Latin alphabet to write in English, we have twenty-six letters but more than forty sounds—so "we have letters doing 'doubletime'" (Curzan, "Spelling" 143). That complicates spelling.

- Sometimes words have changed in pronunciation but not in spelling—so the spelling reflects the older way of speaking, as in words like *knight*.

- Because of interest in classical periods, "Renaissance scholars sometimes made efforts to change English spelling to conform to the Latin forms of the words" that English had borrowed from French, as in *debt* (Curzan, "Spelling" 144).

- Borrowing from other languages, something English does often, complicates spelling because those words don't follow English spelling patterns either. In some cases, there's even double borrowing, further complicating spelling issues; *colonel* is one example of this, borrowed from both French and Italian so that we have the French pronunciation and Italian spelling.

- Then, we should add, there is Noah Webster, who wanted to use American spellings as a way to reinforce independence from England—so we have some spelling changes (e.g., *theater* instead of *theatre*) from that period and some spellings that stayed the same as England's.

Still, Crystal estimates that "80 percent of the English lexicon is spelled according to regular patterns, and only 3 percent is so irregular that speakers must learn the spellings individually" (qtd. in Curzan, "Spelling" 142), so the problem with spelling isn't insurmountable. Knowing the history of the language at least makes it understandable (see Table 1.1).

As students address ideas of language change, it's only natural that they should confront ways that some users of language manipulate it to their advantage. Because many advertisements use language in persuasive ways that students might be unaware of, exploring connotation and denotation of words is an important aspect of being a critical reader and a critical viewer. Recognizing this aspect of language is an essential part of understanding language change, especially as it affects critical thinking among consumers and citizens in a democracy. As Alvarez reminds us:

> Misusing the language is something that dictatorships and totalitarian governments know all about. One of the first things such a regime does is to seize control of the media, to sensor the stories of the people, to silence dissenting opinions. I grew up where there was only one story—the official story. In the dictatorship of Rafael Leonida Trujillo in the Dominican Republic, 1930–1961, books were rewritten to tell his truth, and his truth only on pain of death. In a school not far away from where I attended classes, a young teacher corrected a student's essay on Trujillo by suggesting that there had been other "liberators" of the country. That night, the teacher, his wife, and two children disappeared. (39)

As teachers, we can help students understand this aspect of language change when we have them read and analyze political speeches (past and present) as well as advertisements and op-eds. When students are aware of the difference between denotation and connotation, when they understand how words can shape attitudes and feelings, they can show responsible use of that knowledge in their own reading and writing for public purposes.

Extending Your Knowledge

Darren Crovitz and Michelle Devereaux encourage teachers to help students understand how language is used in the public sphere, particularly how it can be manipulated to reflect "underlying stances and ideologies" (31). They provide several language experiences for teachers to use with their students to help develop students' critical thinking. Helping students understand that the placement of noun phrases, the use of passive voice, or the use of participial phrases to shape meaning in subtle ways are all valuable in helping students see how grammar matters in their understanding of the world.

The idea that words have meanings that can be manipulated is only one part of language change. In his preface to the new translation of *Night*, Elie Wiesel addresses another aspect of language that students should understand: language changes when our words become inadequate to express human emotions or conditions. As he writes:

> I had many things to say, I did not have the words to say them. Painfully aware of my limitations, I watched helplessly as language became an obstacle. It became clear that it would be necessary to invent a new language. But how was one to rehabilitate and transform words betrayed and perverted by the enemy? Hunger—thirst—fear—transport—selection—fire—chimney: these words all have intrinsic meaning, but in those times, they meant something else. Writing in my mother tongue—at that point close to extinction—I would pause at every sentence, and start over and over again. I would conjure up other verbs, other images, other silent cries. It still was not right. But what exactly was "it"? It was something elusive, darkly shrouded for fear of being usurped, profaned. All the dictionary had to offer seemed meager, pale, lifeless. (ix)

Helping our students appreciate this sensitive issue related to language change is important. There are always words that are changing meanings and words that are shifting in meaning that teachers can ask students to consider as aspects of language change. Some of this happens organically, but some is formalized. In August 2019, the board of supervisors of San Francisco moved to change words allowed in government. Noting that "language shapes the ideas, perceptions, beliefs, attitudes, and actions of individuals, societies, and governments," the board moved to eliminate words like *felon* and *juvenile delinquent* from the criminal justice system ("San Francisco Pushes to Rebrand" par. 7).

Certainly that is a case of language change. When words don't work for us, when they are restricted to certain groups, when they become inadequate because of our experiences, language changes—or society does—to accommodate the needs. If students understand that, they are really learning about grammar and language at its most sensitive levels.

Rhetorical Grammar

This aspect of grammar instruction is probably the most familiar to teachers; it is the grammar that relates to effective (not simply correct) writing, sometimes also called *stylistic grammar*. To me, rhetorical grammar is the way students apply what they know about language at all levels, not only at the level of correctness but also at the level of meaning and sense—abilities they will gain from a language program that treats grammar in all its forms: as parts of speech and editing, yes, but also as variation and usage and meaning. All aspects of language come into play in teaching rhetorical grammar.

Teachers and writers who work with rhetorical grammar (Ehrenworth and Vinton; Marchetti and O'Dell; Ray) promote the use of *mentor texts*, pieces of writing that students can read for ideas to implement in their own writing. I like the term *mentor* rather than *model*, an older term for the same concept, because of the implications. Mentors guide, advise, and support; models are a likeness, pattern, or copy. I want the texts that my students study to serve as possibilities, not constraints. Teaching students how to use them as such is important for their learning rhetorical grammar, so showing them how to question, consider, and choose when to use ideas from mentor texts is an important part of teacher work. Having students use and then reflect on the effects of their language choices in their writing is also the key to developing their rhetorical grammar.

Schuster relies heavily on professional texts as a way to learn which rules of writing really matter. In sampling published writing, students (and the teacher) investigate what constitutes effective writing. For example, in exploring the admonition to vary sentence beginnings, Schuster examined numerous classic and modern essays to conclude that "the advice to vary sentence openings is very bad advice indeed. Professional writers open sentences with their subjects approximately two thirds of the time" (*Breaking* 122). Tufte's assessment is the same: two thirds of English sentences begin with the subject, and about one quarter begin with an adverbial construction. Not a lot of variety. Students can use mentor texts to investigate all aspects of language use: usage, conventions, dialects, genre, and more.

Sentence imitation and sentence combining are other ways to learn rhetorical grammar that also come from mentor texts. Students imitate the structure of mentor sentences with their own content. Usually this helps extend students' repertoire of grammatical structures. Depending on the mentor sentences, students can learn how to use appositives, participial phrases, subordinate clauses, or parallel structure (among many other possible structures) in their writing. They don't have to know the names of the structures—in fact, I started teaching imitation by naming the parts of the sentence ("The sentence starts with an infinitive phrase . . .") and just about destroyed my students' interest before I learned that they could imitate without naming anything. Once they understood the idea of imitation, they became avid imitators, bringing in sentences for me to use with the class and sharing their imitations generously. Sometimes they didn't always use them effectively in their writing, failing to match the structure to the tone of the writing, as one girl did who wrote about skateboarding while imitating many sentences from former US President John F. Kennedy's Inaugural Address. To me, that is part of the learning process, and she, like others, figured out what needed to be done to make sentences rhetorically as well as structurally effective.

Sentence combining can contribute to students' learning of rhetorical grammar in similar ways. Despite some resistance to it during the 1970s and 1980s, sentence combining is one of eleven instructional methods that has research supporting its effectiveness (Graham and Perin). Students combine short kernel sentences into longer sentences, either with cues or without. The combining activity should encourage students to consider a variety of ways to arrange the content of a sentence and the effects of different arrangements. The challenge with sentence combining is that many teachers fail to use it in the way that will actually benefit students. Instead, they often focus on correctness or on matching the original sentence that the kernels developed from. Instead, I ask students to combine the kernel sentences in at least two different ways so that they are pushed to consider more than the default option that comes first. Students choose the combination they like best and consider why they like it. When we share, I ask for responses from several students so that we can discuss the effects of combining one way over another: Why do they like one sentence more than another? What difference in meaning do the various combinations create? This work with sentences should *not* be about right and wrong; it's about rhetorical effectiveness and helping students understand how they might achieve it.

In addition to sentence combining and sentence imitation, Johnson advocates lessons on stylistic devices; lessons that, he argues, help students not only revise their writing but also generate new ideas about their topics. Johnson explains that "stylistic devices are not merely *fun*, not just toys for writers, but tools by which writers can create certain effects on readers, physical feelings of comprehension and power, knowledge and connection" (37). He uses mini-lessons and exercises to acquaint students with devices of rhythm and balance and sound (e.g., asyndeton, antithesis, alliteration), but, he explains, his purpose is not to get students to write "heavily stylized language" (40). Instead, Johnson wants them to "practice these devices as a kind of interim measure toward listening to and thinking about their prose more carefully" (40). His ultimate goal is for students to feel a sort of pleasure from their writing and to become more confident thought "participant(s) in the world" (61). I've tried some of his methods, too, and found that my students gained a better awareness of what language can do and what they can do with it—just what we want from rhetorical grammar.

Well, that's my list and my explanations. I'm well aware that there are problems inherent in presenting any type of schema for a subject as broad as this is. Some might disagree with my choices; that's okay. At least that means we're all thinking about teaching language and what it means and what students need. One limitation to the schema I've presented is how it plays out when I talk about it in this book. It's hard to separate grammar integrated with reading completely from grammar for writing or speaking. It seems that, as we work with language during reading, students will gain knowledge that could—and should—find its way into their writing and speaking—and vice versa. So the chapter divisions I present artificially separate what wouldn't be separated in the classroom. I hope readers can see that these chapters peer more deeply into what's seen on the surface in the classroom dialogues that thread through the book. That's how they were meant to be seen.

Questions for Reflection

1. If you had to decide which aspects of grammar would be taught, what would be on your list? How would it differ from the list presented in this chapter? What rationale do you have for your own list?

2. What are some ways you can already envision integrating these aspects into your own classroom? How do you see this integration benefiting your students?

3. What do you need to do to prepare to integrate the aspects you would like to use but don't know enough about? Make a plan (a list of readings, a timeline, a suggestion for courses to take) for how you will accomplish your preparation.

2

Writing and Language

We seduce the students into grammar. We let grammar seduce us. We assume that it is, in fact, seductive, and we search out those writers who manipulate and exploit grammatical structures in their writing.

—*Mary Ehrenworth*

I had believed what I read: teaching grammar was useful in helping writers "fix" their mistakes in writing. I knew the admonitions about connecting grammar instruction with writing, but the only place people talked about the connection seemed to be with the last part of writing, with editing. It just seemed logical to me that knowing about language could influence what comes before editing, when we are actually putting the first words on the paper, maybe even before that—when we are shaping ideas in our heads? I was a little uncomfortable with the limitation, but, as a new teacher, what did I know?

Since my early questioning, I've found others who've wondered the same thing: Umbach, speaking of the way handbooks present grammar, explains that "the message is clear. Grammar is what you use to clean up the mess that you make, that you will inevitably make" (5). Ah. So, even if we don't connect grammar to writing, if we do it only as a way to "clean up" writing, what message does that send about grammar and language? And why would students be motivated to learn much about it? After all, autocorrect can pick up a lot of those messes.

Should grammar—language—have an impact on the whole writing process? It seems that it should help writers know the level of language to use with certain genres. Burke agrees: "The more a student understands [how language works], the more options he or she has when starting to write" ("Developing" 57). Ehrenworth and Vinton see grammar/language as contributing to voice in writing: "If, as we believe, grammar is linked to voice, students need to be thinking about grammar far earlier in the writing process" (10). Since voice is woven into the writing, not added on at the end, it makes sense to consider how lessons on language might benefit writers earlier in the writing process.

Let's look into a classroom to consider how this might look:

TEACHER: We've read *The House on Mango Street* and talked about its themes and ideas. As we read, we also discussed some ideas about how Cisneros has created her unique voice and how that voice added to the messages of the book. I'd like us to go back and look at some of the chapters in a little more detail. Let's start with the chapter titled "My Name," on pages 10 and 11. Let's read it again, looking a little more in depth at what it's doing and how it works. Sarah, will you please read the first paragraph aloud while we all follow along? Thanks!

TEACHER (*after Sarah's reading*): Great! Thanks. What are some language uses you notice in this paragraph?

SEAN: She broke a bunch of rules. I want to do that. Can I do that in this writing?

TEACHER: Let's talk about it. What "rules" are you referring to, Sean?

SEAN: For one thing, starting sentences with the same word: *it, it, it.*

TEACHER: Okay. What is the "rule"?

SEAN: My teacher last year made us list all the first words of sentences in a list and then make sure they were all different. So . . . no repeating.

TEACHER: Why do you think teachers might encourage variety of sentence beginnings? Anyone?

MELANIE: Probably to keep writing interesting, to keep it from being boring?

SEAN: To give me something else to worry about. (*Class laughs.*)

TEACHER: Okay, why would Cisneros use it repeatedly here? What is she thinking it will do for her writing, for her readers? I think we have to assume she knows the "rule," as Sean calls it.

MARIE: Well, at least in those two short sentences, it—I mean the word *it* at the beginning—kind of makes the sentence more about the ending words, *sadness* and *waiting*.

ELTON: Yeah, it does. And it works even in the later one. It makes us focus on *Mexican records*.

TEACHER: Okay. So what might we say about the use of the same word at the beginning of multiple sentences? (*After a pause.*) Can we make a better "rule" for this than just use a different word every time?

ELLE: What about only using or repeating a beginning word if it makes us focus on the last part of the sentence more?

TEACHER: What do the rest of you think? Is that a good way to think about it?

(*Some nodding.*)

GABE: What if we *don't* want people to pay more attention to the end of the sentence? What if want them to pay attention to something else?

MARIE: Well, I don't think you should use the same word at the beginning.

TEACHER: Do you think the word at the beginning matters? I mean, what if it's something other than *it*?

MARIE: I do. But I think it has to be something important for us to say over and over—not just any word. If we want people to pay attention, it just seems like we shouldn't ask them to pay attention to something that isn't important.

SEAN: So, if the word is important, maybe I *could* use it at the beginning of some sentences in a row?

TEACHER: What do the rest of you think?

GABRIELLE: I think it could work, but we'd have to think about the word, that it was important.

TEACHER: Good point, Gabrielle. What other language uses did you notice in this piece of writing that stood out for you, that made it effective?

ITZEL: I noticed some short sentences. Some really short, like one word long.

TEACHER: Good eye. Can some of you tell me what those short sentences are?

SPENCER: "A muddy color." "My great-grandmother." The first time I read that one, I was thinking, "What about her?"

SHAYE: Yes. I mean, there is a sentence that is only "yes." (*Some chuckles.*) And her name is all by itself in a sentence: "Esperanza."

TEACHER: Good noticings. Let's think about why Cisneros would make this choice.

SEAN: She gets to break all the rules!

TEACHER: Well, writers, if they are trying to create an effect, can choose to use fragments. She actually has some longer fragments, too. Let's see if you can find those, too, to consider why writers use them. Work with a partner for a few minutes to see what you can find, since these are a little harder to notice.

(*After a few minutes.*)

TEACHER: Okay. Maria, I asked you to share one you found with Sarah. What is it?

MARIA: "Until my great-grandfather threw a sack over her head and carried her off."

TEACHER: Good find! Why did you identify it as a fragment?

MARIA: Because it just felt like it wasn't whole, like it was really part of the sentence before it.

TEACHER. Okay—and that's one reason we see writers use fragments—to set off a part of a sentence by itself. Why do you think they do that? Why not keep it combined?

AUSTIN: Maybe, when it's by itself, it's kinda like more important or something, like it's something to think about all by itself?

TEACHER: I think that's a great insight, Austin. Maybe we can use this as one "rule" for fragments? (*Writing on a wall chart.*) "A part of a sentence that we want to set off by itself to increase the reader's focus on it." Does that work? (*Murmurs of assent.*) What cautions would we have to consider? Would this be a good thing to do all the time?

SPENCER: If you did it all the time, it seems like it would be weird. Like no flow or something.

BARRETT: Yeah, all bumpy.

TEACHER: Good to consider. What about other long fragments? I think I heard you and Abby had one you found, Elise.

ELISE: We thought there was another one in the last paragraph: "Esperanza as Lisandra or Martiza or Zeze the X."

TEACHER: Did you come up with any theories about why Cisneros would use a fragment there?

ELISE: We thought maybe to kind of focus on the other names she'd like? To emphasize them?

TEACHER: Okay—so fragments draw our attention? Does that work for the other ones, the shorter ones we found earlier? (*Murmurs of assent.*) Then what might we make up for another rule for fragments? How can we say it?

ABBY: Maybe if we want to make sure to emphasize something, to get readers to focus on something?

TEACHER: Does that work for everyone? Okay, so rule number 2 would be "to emphasize or focus"? (*Murmurs of assent.*)

TEACHER (*as she writes it on wall chart*): Okay, then, we have two "rules" for when we could use fragments. Do we have a caution for this one?

BARRETT: Well, it seems like, if you make everything a focus, then nothing is.

SEAN: Yeah. I guess I can't just go using them all the time or my reader wouldn't know what to focus on. But it seems like I would like to use them all the time 'cause they kind of sound like how we talk.

TEACHER: Good point, Sean. We often speak in fragments, don't we? So we could consider that—"as a way for our writing to sound more informal, more like speech"—as another rule? Do we have a third one now? (*Writing it on wall chart.*) Are there any cautions for this one?

SARAH: Well, if it's school writing, like a report or something, maybe we shouldn't make it sound like we're just talking. Maybe it should sound smarter? (*Some chuckles.*)

TEACHER: I know what you mean, Sarah. It does seem like the writing we often do for school—academic writing—doesn't sound much like conversation, does it? One thing we could consider is looking at our mentor texts—remember how we've done that for figuring out a new genre and what it allows us to do? Maybe we could look at those mentor texts for whether fragments or informal sentence structures would work for the kind of writing we are doing? Does that sound doable? Okay, then, if we do that, and we are going to write about our own names. (*Some groans.*)

SEAN: I *knew* that was coming!

TEACHER: . . . so, if we write about our own names, would you say fragments are going to be okay? (*Murmurs of agreement.*) Within reason?

TEACHER: Okay, then. Now that you know what we're going to be doing here in a minute, what else about the language should we notice to consider as options for our own writing? Anything else?

TEACHER: In the next few weeks, we are going to be writing some vignettes of our own, in the same manner as Cisneros, to share some insights into our own lives and the lenses through which we see the world. Now, Sean, this will be fun! I really look forward to hearing your voices and your thoughts about the world. Let's start with some freewriting about your name. We'll do some other inquiry to enrich our writing, but, for now, try to get into the mood of this writing by writing for a few minutes about your name: Do you like it? Why or why not? Are you named after someone? If so, are you happy about that or not? What does your name sound like? Do you have a nickname? Whatever comes to mind, okay? And go ahead and think about using fragments or repeating first words or other grammar you noticed that works for your writing. Good? Let's go.

Did we do our students a disservice when we thought we were doing better by connecting grammar to editing? If we have made the connection only as a remediation strategy, it's not surprising that students would still see grammar as unfamiliar and unpleasant. When we teach grammar in isolation, students might think they "know" grammar, but they probably can't translate their understanding into improved writing. If, instead, we teach grammar as part of the entire writing process, if we use Myhill et al.'s recommendations (summarized in the following paragraphs) to teach grammar as choice, we can position the writers in our classes as "agentive, creative shapers of meaning, designing texts in terms of ideas, layout, voice and including grammatical choice" (104).

Myhill et al. recommend the following ideas for implementing effective "grammar in the context of writing" instruction:

- Grammatical terms are used but explained through examples rather than by definition—and are not the focus of lessons. Some instructors feel that students don't need to know terms, and it's true they don't need them for writing. But sometimes a few terms make conversation about writing easier. The key is to have students learn the concept before the term and apply the concept in writing right away—then use the term in talking about the writing—instead of starting with a term and definition.

- Teachers make clear connections between the language element studied and its application to current writing. Much of this has to do with students and teachers talking about the effects of the language elements they study: Why have a short sentence here? Why use an appositive instead of a subordinate clause? Myhill et al. note that teachers should consider talk as a "key mechanism" for learning about language (106).
- Students learn to use imitation and sentence combining in playful ways to build options for their writing. The practice with these activities should encourage risk-taking, which means they can't be graded. Instead, these activities should help students learn options they have for their own writing, and they work best when mentor texts are from the real world so that students see how their writing connects to the world outside of school.
- Teachers need to ensure that classroom activities and assignments encourage students to see themselves as writers who make choices. This means that they write the kinds of texts that exist in the world, ones that have room for writers to sometimes make mistakes or sometimes excel beyond their expectations. They shouldn't be limited to the kinds of texts that usually inhabit classrooms that restrict choices and options.

Teaching grammar with writing does appear to improve writing. Research confirms that "teaching students to focus on the function and practical application of grammar within the context of writing . . . produced strong and positive effects on students' writing" (Graham and Perin 21). An understanding of grammar can improve student writing, but it should be taught in a way that makes sense to the learners and seems useful to them so that they will be encouraged to transfer their learning to other writing situations.

Traditional Grammar

Creating Cinquain Poems

Poetry is an effective way to build students' understanding of traditional grammar through writing. Many poetic forms require students to use specific parts of speech, but all poetry focuses on language—its denotative and connotative meanings as well as its metaphorical and symbolic uses. The enlarged perspective of language that students can gain from writing poetry is beneficial in numerous ways to their growing understanding of language.

1. Begin by teaching students the form of the poem. *Cinquain* poems are poems with five lines that allow students to write poetry at the same time as they use their knowledge of parts of speech. In this form, the first line is a noun that announces the subject (and title) of the poem. The second line consists of two adjectives that describe the noun. Line 3 consists of three verbs in the *-ing* form. Line 4 differentiates between phrases and clauses by requiring a phrase that represents a feeling, image, or metaphor about the subject. Line 5 is a single noun, a synonym for the first line or subject of the poem.

2. To complete the poems, students need to know the ideas of parts of speech and the ideas of phrases and clauses—even if they can't name them or define them in traditional grammar terms. Seeing models helps my students, who otherwise would be confused, to know what I mean by the terms I use to explain the writing. There are many models on the internet (just type in "cinquain"). Show students the models and talk about them enough so that students understand the concepts; then have them write one or two of their own and share them. Here is my example:

> Alaska
> Enormous, Empty
> Freezing, Flowing, Quaking
> Land of the Midnight Sun
> Home

Alternative Suggestion: Other poetic forms can also help students learn about traditional grammar concepts—if not the terms themselves. *Diamante* poems work like cinquains except that they have two more lines (duplicating parts but not the content of the second and third line after the phrase line). Weaver uses "I Am" poems to help students learn participial phrases (*Teaching Grammar* 214–17). The poems begin with a metaphor in the first line, with each subsequent line beginning with a participial phrase, an *-ing* verb form, describing how the metaphor works. Most poems have three or four such lines after the first one. I show students models of the poetic form and discuss with them what they see and what they understand about the poems and the form. They see from the examples that some of these poems can be concrete; others are more abstract, as shown in this example from Weaver's book:

> I am a strong lasting tool
> Nailing friends together
> Pounding kindness into the world

Sawing through problems

Sanding rough edges in life. (*Teaching Grammar* 216)

Students write these "I Am" poems about themselves, about characters in books they are reading, or about concepts they are studying. A preservice teacher, Tonya Hamill, adapted the concept to a lesson on metaphors and similes by having her students identify the metaphors in art by Vladimir Kush and then explain those metaphors in poems built with participial phrases. In Tonya's lesson, students were learning a literary concept, using writing to explore their ideas and thinking, and learning about grammar—all at once.

Other poetic forms that can help students learn traditional grammar concepts or terms include the following (all explained very nicely with examples in Judy Young's *R Is for Rhyme: A Poetry Alphabet*):

- *Doublets* are poems built around a word ladder—words in a list, each word one letter different from the word before. The form encourages creativity with and sensitivity to words.

- *Haiku* poems require sensitivity to imagery and language. Examples from *If Not for the Cat* (Prelutsky) can help students see how adjectives and adverbs can be used effectively in this poetic form.

- *Rap* poetry encourages students to play with language and rhythm in ways that help them learn about grammar as they try to make meaning in rhythmic language.

Writing from Different Perspectives

Another way I use writing to help students learn traditional grammar concepts is when I have them rewrite a scene or story, but from different perspectives.

1. Begin by retelling familiar childhood stories such as "The Three Bears" or "The Three Pigs" from the perspectives of different characters in the stories. In these oral retellings, students practice shifts in stance that they can apply when they write their own experience from different perspectives. This gives them practice with using first person (I/we/me) and third person (they/he/she/them).

2. Have students choose an event that they attended with at least a few other people: a football game, a concert, a movie, and so forth. Initially, have them write a first-person account, as this allows them to review the event

in what (for my students at least) is the most comfortable perspective to retell an event. I tell them that this means they have to use *I*, *we*, and *me*.

3. After they complete the first-person draft, have them rewrite the event in the third person. Discuss what this means orally first so that students understand that not only do we shift pronouns, but we also have to consider other aspects of the event ("What would others see and experience that I didn't?"). Then have students write the second version of the event.

4. When students have finished their two versions, have them compare and contrast them in small- or whole-class discussion. What differences do they notice? Students discover that shifting perspective changes the information selected and the stance toward that information. More than that, though, they should see that the different stance creates a different tone—first person is more immediate and personal while third person is more distant and impersonal.

5. With this foundation about the effects of pronoun choice laid, have students investigate different genres that are traditionally written in first or third person. News articles, for instance, are written in third person, as are traditional research papers. Letters, however, are written in first person. Even business letters, which are more formal than personal letters, aren't as objective and distant as news articles or research articles. Students should discover that the genres use the different perspectives for a reason—those perspectives are part of each genre's situation and purpose.

6. Next, have students rewrite selected genres from a different perspective. This will teach them about writing and genre while they learn about language. For instance, when they rewrite a news article with a first-person perspective, they can see what is lost and what is gained. Personal letters written from a third-person stance (this can be tricky) lose something that makes a letter meaningful. After students write these genres from an alternate stance, lead them in a discussion about how stance is related to the genre and the situation in which the genre is acting. Although there are variations in genres, students can build awareness of traditional grammar (pronouns) not only as parts of speech but also as related to the effects they create in writing different genres.

Alternative Suggestion: In a similar way, Burke suggests having students rewrite text passages—either published ones or their own—in a different verb tense, to see the resulting effect. As he notes, "Such exercises help students to understand how language functions to orient the reader in time, and to create different perspectives on the same story or subject" ("Developing" 59). Ehrenworth and Vinton agree and suggest reading literature by authors such as Sandra Cisneros for things like examples in verb tense to see how Cisneros creates voice and point of view. As they note, "It is hopeless to ask students to memorize verb forms, especially irregular verb endings, until they see the choice of verb tense as a meaningful one" (69). Again, the shift in grammar creates resultant shifts in tone and position that readers should notice and writers can emulate when necessary.

Editing

Punctuating for Meaning

In *Image Grammar: Using Grammatical Structures to Teach Writing*, Noden remarks that, for "most authors, meaning takes precedence over rules" when it comes to punctuation (98). Iyer represents this idea in his description of punctuation as guides, not as rules:

> Punctuation marks are the road signs placed along the highway of our communication—to control speeds, provide directions, and prevent head-on collisions. A period has the unblinking finality of a red light; the comma is a flashing yellow light that asks us only to slow down; and the semicolon is a stop sign that tells us to ease gradually to a halt, before gradually starting up again. By establishing the relations between words, punctuation establishes the relations between the people using words. (93–94)

Helping students see punctuation as road signs, as meaning-making, benefits them as readers and writers—and, in the long run, helps students understand how their own choices as writers can benefit readers, or make it harder to understand what they are trying to communicate.

1. Begin by reading with students the following passage from a short story by Adam Schwartz (shared by Bomer). Help students develop their understanding of how punctuation can assist readers by having them imagine the phrasing created by the commas in the sentence. Here's the original text:

   > I told her I knew she might be disappointed, but I wasn't rejecting her; I only wanted to spend more time with my father, to know and love him as well as I knew her. (528)

2. In his rewriting of this passage, Bomer punctuates the sentence to show that "to figure out what sentences are saying, we have to hear the words (in our mind's ear) together in the appropriate phrasing" (529). What follows is Bomer's re-punctuated version:

> I told her. I knew she might. Be disappointed. But I wasn't rejecting. Her I only wanted to spend. More time with my father to know? And love him as well as I knew her. (529)

Ask students what they notice. How does the re-punctuation make communication harder? Students will see the obvious: punctuation can make a big difference in communicating effectively. It isn't only about "right" and "wrong."

3. Next, speak sentences or passages you have prepared and have students punctuate them so that another person reading the printed text would read it as we said it. For example, how might a writer punctuate this sentence so that a sense of frustration (or even threat) is evident in the written text?

> "I haven't gotten to you [*pause*] yet."

Students could write it this way: "I haven't gotten to you yet." But that doesn't suggest the pause at all. They could write: "I haven't gotten to you, but I will eventually." Different words, but the message is closer to our intent. What about "I haven't gotten to you—yet." Better. How is this version—"I haven't gotten to you. Yet."—different? Is it more interesting? Have students discuss how they can use punctuation to make meaning clear. Find sentences in conversations or in movies and take them to class to use in explorations like this one. This activity helps students get practice in making editing choices that guide readers and that make punctuation a contributor to meaning, not just an application of rules.

Extending Your Knowledge

Tom Romano, an advocate of alternate style and personal voice, still recognizes the value of conventional correctness: "I also want [students] to realize that, if their writing is a mechanical disaster, their natural voice might be dismissed by others, regardless of how authentic, colorful, and pointed it is" (73). Punctuation matters!

Using Mentor Texts to Help Students Infer Reader Expectations for Punctuation

When my students have trouble with conventions that interfere with my reading of their writing—and these problems are not a result of trying to make meaning but more a result of failing to consider reader expectations—I find sentences that exemplify the conventions I want my students to edit for, sentences that help them know that readers read punctuation like road signs. If writers put up a stop sign when they want the reader only to slow down, that's a problem.

1. Find examples of the punctuation challenges students are having in texts you read. For example, I noticed that my students' writing had distracted me because of their use (or, rather, the lack of use) of commas with long introductory elements and in compound sentences. When I read the book *Sitting Ducks* (Bedard), I realized it would help my students learn reader expectations for commas in these constructions. I read the book to them and used sentences from the text for a mini-lesson. I gave students three sets of sentences and asked them to tell me what they could learn about comma use from the examples. The following is an abbreviated sample set:

    > But one day, an egg came through the incubation chamber unhatched.
    > Dazed by this rude introduction into the world, a little duck emerged and surveyed his strange surroundings.

    > He just had to sneak away and explore the streets below.
    > He rushed in and hopped up onto a stool.

    > At first, the alligator was bewildered by this weird welcome, but soon he joined in the crazy dance.
    > They even tried going out together, but it proved to be very awkward.

    The students infer, correctly, that they should use commas after introductory elements and between independent clauses (although they didn't use those terms) but not if the second part of the sentence wasn't a "whole sentence."

2. Next, have students return to their writing and implement what they have learned about punctuation for reader expectation. Encourage students to pay attention to punctuation when they read so that they become familiar with reader expectations about punctuation. There is only one caution— and that is that some writers don't always follow the "rules." Sometimes that is because expectations change over time, and an author's punctuation may have been appropriate for the time period in which the text was writ-

ten but isn't now. Sometimes different genres have differing expectations for punctuation. It's good to teach students that punctuation rules change through time and among genres—a helpful and useful thing to know. But some alternate use of punctuation goes back to meaning: sometimes writers use unexpected punctuation to draw attention to an idea.

By not doing what's expected, readers have to slow down, pay attention, and interpret. For example, using the following paragraph from Wiesel's essay "Why I Write: Making No Become Yes," draw students' attention to the three compound sentences listed below the paragraph, each of which is punctuated differently.

> Where was I to discover a fresh vocabulary, a primeval language? The language of night was not human, it was primitive, almost animal—hoarse shouting, screams, muffled moaning, savage howling, the sound of beating. A brute strikes out wildly, a body falls. An officer raises his arm and a whole community walks toward a common grave. A soldier shrugs his shoulders, and a thousand families are torn apart, to be reunited only by death. This was the concentration camp language. (23)
>
> A brute strikes out wildly, a body falls.
>
> An officer raises his arm and a whole community walks toward a common grave.
>
> A soldier shrugs his shoulders, and a thousand families are torn apart, to be reunited only by death.

After reading the paragraph and paying specific attention to these three sentences, ask students why Wiesel might have used commas in both expected and unexpected ways, remembering that meaning is enhanced by punctuation. My students' answers astound me with their insight. With regard to unexpected punctuation use, students should also realize, however, that being a student writer and being a published writer are two different things. Sometimes readers have different expectations of each type of writer. It's not particularly fair; it's just how things are.

Usage

Writing Letters to Different Audiences

In working with children of agricultural laborers in his classroom, Shafer found that traditional lessons on usage and language didn't engage his students.

He learned that language lessons needed to be a part of "authentic language experiences that directly touched the lives" of his students (38). Interestingly, instead of simply teaching usage as a standard, which is how some teachers might approach such a situation—even if teaching grammar in the context of writing—he taught language as flexible, as responsive to situation. Dunn and Lindblom assert that a flexible approach is more effective:

> To combat these barriers to upward mobility, students do not need to know "the rules" for writing successfully. What they need is the ability to communicate effectively with people in all kinds of contexts for all kinds of purposes. Pretending that grammar rules provide a smooth, toll-free road to economic success is a harmful myth. ("Why" 45)

Barret extends this argument: "Although it is certainly true that there are contexts in which the grammatical function of Standard English is indispensable, there are also contexts in which knowledge of other dialects is critical for 'wider' communication to occur" (Young et al. 49). For Shafer, teaching effective communication reflects these ideas: "Each assignment would, then, probe the worthiness of the language used and the reason why it was successful" (39). The following lesson idea adapts Shafer's teaching.

1. Have students start by writing a short letter to a friend or relative, one that they will read in class but that is a legitimate letter—one they will actually give or send to the person. After they have written their letters, have students share them as a way to begin to understand how language responds to situation. Have students look for usage that is unique to the relationship—for example, shortcuts of language or signal words that might not mean the same thing outside of the relationship. Students should definitely note the informal usage that is more like speech that often pervades letters to friends or family.

2. Next, have students write a letter to a more formal, outside audience. Shafer had his students write to a prospective employer. I have had my students write to businesses to complain about or compliment products or services (Dean, "Going Public"). Either way, students first need to analyze the situation and consider the audience: How is this audience different from the one they had previously written to? What do those differences entail in terms of language? As students work through the writing process on these letters, they explore the answers to these questions.

3. After writing, discuss with students what they can learn from these two writing experiences. When they realized the different levels of usage that were expected in the different situations, Shafer explains that his students "discussed the place of power and the way it tends to define what is 'standard' or 'correct'" (40). Teachers have hopes that helping students move away from the right/wrong dichotomy to a consideration of appropriateness could help diminish the alienation students might feel about their home languages. However, Barret asserts that "the end result does not seem to be very different" (Young et al. 51). What teachers might do to accommodate a more flexible approach could include helping students understand the degree to which each letter allows for variations away from the expectations for Standard English as they understand it. For instance, they could take copies of the two letters and highlight any variations from the standard they see and compare the percentages and the kinds of variations. In that way, students could understand that the use of language is more like a sliding scale than an either/or usage.

Extending Your Knowledge

In discussing his own usage practices, Edwin Battistella notes that "my usage follows long habit that I have had no social reason to change" (18). If our students have had no social repercussions for using their informal usage, what does that tell them about "rules" and the social nature of usage? If they see situations where repercussions may occur— and if those situations matter to them—then they will have more motivation to pay attention to the usage expectations of those situations. Our instruction could prepare them for any necessary shifts they may need to make.

Analyzing Grammar Rants

Grammar rants are found all around us. They are writers' observations and opinions about language, usually focusing on some aspect the writer finds interesting or bothersome. The bestseller *Eats, Shoots and Leaves: The Zero Tolerance Approach to Punctuation* (Truss) might be considered a lengthy grammar rant—the introduction is definitely one. Dunn and Lindblom explain how analyzing grammar rants can help develop savvy writers: "Savvy writers know the conventions of genre, their own levels of power in each writing situation, and the expectations of their audience. Analyzing grammar rants can heighten the skills necessary for savvy writing" ("Grammar" xiii). To Dunn and Lindblom's suggestions for analyzing grammar rants, I add a writing component to encourage reflection and longer-lasting learning. Here's how I teach their idea.

1. To prepare students for the world of grammar rants, share with them the satirical rant "What Is and Ain't Grammatical" (Barry). In this essay, Barry raises (in a humorous way) some of the issues underlying grammar rants. I use the essay to start a discussion about attitudes toward grammar so that the rants students read later have some context.

2. Next, provide students with some grammar rants. Have students work in pairs and read the rants. These rants can be found all over the internet, in blogs, or on the websites for journals or newspapers. Some sites even have regular language columns that could be used for this activity, or teachers could conduct online searches for "grammar rants." As students read, ask them to look for the following points:

   - the "problem(s)" about which the writer is ranting
   - what the writer sees as the problem with the "problem"
   - why the writer is so unhappy about the "problem"

   As students read and discuss their articles, encourage them to place the rants in a larger, cultural context. What does it say about language and people that there are writers who write about these issues? When students share their findings with the whole class, help them see that usage issues (most often the subject of the rants) have more overtones as well as implications about power and relationships.

3. Next, using Schuster's suggestion of analyzing the way language is actually used, have students hunt for examples of published writing that violates the "rules" that were the subject of the rants. When they have some evidence (and it's all around us), have them work in their same partnerships to write a rebuttal to the rant. In this rebuttal, they can cite the places and authors that "break the rule" to show that usage expectations are situational or that they change over time. I agree with Dunn and Lindblom that analyzing grammar rants (and researching the subject of the rant so that students can respond to the charges) can "make both teachers and students more sensitive to the particular pet peeves of professional and amateur grammar guardians everywhere, making students more careful shapers of language for each rhetorical situation" ("Developing" 203). When students respond to the rants with "rants" of their own, they develop as critical thinkers about language.

Writing Stories to Develop Language Awareness

Usage often relies on students' hearing. We can aid students in acquiring an "ear" for standard usage with their own talk in the classroom by calling attention to the differences between informal and formal usages in the texts that we read aloud in class. One way to generate texts for students to practice different varieties of usage with is to have them write the stories of wordless picture books. Figure 2.1 lists some titles that work for this practice.

1. Have students work in pairs first to "read" the pictures and develop the general plot of the book they have selected, using talk before writing to create the basics of the story line. Fravel believes that talking "plays a crucial role and impacts the writing of all students regardless of their native language because language acquisition depends on social interaction"

Armstrong, Jennifer. *Once Upon a Banana*. Simon and Schuster, 2006.
Blake, Quentin. *Clown*. Henry Holt, 1995.
Boyd, Lizi. *Flashlight*. Chronicle, 2014.
Briggs, Raymond. *The Snowman*. Random House, 1978.
Cole, Henry. *One Little Bag: An Amazing Journey*. Scholastic, 2020.
Collington, Peter. *The Tooth Fairy*. Knopf, 1995.
Day, Alexandra. *Carl Goes Shopping*. HarperCollins, 1989.
Ludy, Mark. *The Flower Man*. Green Pastures, 2005.
Macaulay, David. *Black and White*. Walter Lorraine, 2005.
Melling, David. *The Ghost Library*. Barrons, 2004.
Priceman, Marjorie. *Hot Air: The (Mostly) True Story of the First Hot-Air Balloon Ride*. Atheneum, 2005.
Rogers, Gregory. *The Boy, the Bear, the Baron, the Bard*. Roaring Brook, 2004.
Teague, Mark. *Fly!* Beach Lane, 2019.
Thompson, Bill. *Chalk*. Two Lions, 2010.
Weisner, David. *Flotsam*. Houghton Mifflin, 2006.
--- *Free Fall*. HarperTrophy, 1988.
--- *Sector 7*. Clarion, 1999.
--- *Tuesday*. Clarion, 2011.
Weitzman, Jacqueline Preiss. *You Can't Take a Balloon into the Metropolitan Museum.*, Dial Books for Young Readers, 1998.
--- *You Can't Take a Balloon into the National Gallery*. Penguin, 2002.

FIGURE 2.1. Wordless picture books for developing language awareness.

(74). I agree. Talk also prepares students with ideas to write. The wordless picture books provide a frame for the story—but no two finished stories are ever exactly the same—which allows students a chance to focus more on the telling of the story than on developing a plot. As such, they are able to focus on language.

2. Consider requiring students to include both informal and formal language in the story, perhaps using characters' dialogue in informal, speech-like language and narration in more formal usage. In this way, students get to practice a variety of language levels in writing as they tell their stories. They can use novels and picture books as mentor texts if they need help with this dual use of language in the same text.

3. After the stories are written, have students share them in small and large groups. Discussion about the stories should focus on how language was used effectively to tell the stories. Have students reflect on the kinds of usages that are easier for them to write, on how the different levels of usage worked to accomplish different purpose in their stories, and on how they knew to adjust for the different purposes. From this reflection, have students consider other writing situations that have expectations for certain levels of usage, and discuss how they know the expectations and what they can do to achieve them.

Language Change

Writing Advertisements

When students watch advertisements, they may not be attentive to the language being used to influence them or connect to them. When they have to write their own ads, though, they become much more sensitive to language used to connect or to change perceptions and behavior.

1. Begin by having students analyze the language of oral advertisements. I start with oral ads so that students will focus on language more than the visual appeals that play into ads on the various screens they watch. Have students bring in the texts of ads they hear without any reference to the visual elements. Encourage students to find ads that don't mention price directly, that are more subtle in their use of language. Strongly worded promotional ads don't always use the most effective language, relying instead on price or economics as the sales tool: "Call now and we'll throw

in a second ____ absolutely free/with only an additional handling charge."
Some tracks for ads can be found online. For example, the public rela-
tions/news website MultiVu hosts "Beef. It's What's for Dinner" brand
ads from the beef industry that may be familiar to students (National
Livestock and Meat Board). I favor these advertisements because they are
not the typical promotional ads with which students are more familiar. The
language of these ads is used to connect with consumers and to encourage
positive feelings toward the product, not necessarily to sell it. This more
subtle use of language can help students see how effective language can
be used to make connections between consumers and products—and has
nothing to do with economics, which is the aspect of advertising language
our students are more familiar with.

2. When students have scripts for the ads, guide them as they investigate the
   language, specifically looking for the way language is used to persuade
   listeners. They might want to look at the imagery in word choice, the level
   of formality, the use of pronouns, or the use of sentence types (imperative,
   interrogatory, exclamatory, or declarative) as well as the way the words are
   spoken to see how the writers of the ads appeal to their selected audiences.
   Considering the audience should be a major part of this exploration and
   analysis.

   An older ad from the beef industry brand mentioned above included
   this text:

   > Twilight lingers over your backyard. The charcoals turn from black, to red, to
   > white. It's time. Four perfect steaks hit the grill, making a sizzling sound that
   > says, "Summer is here." The cicadas hit their crescendo. They're saying, "Wel-
   > come back, friend. We missed you." The feeling is mutual. Beef. It's what's for
   > dinner.

   The ad uses declarative sentences to describe a scene that writers hope
   will appeal to listeners. The variety of sentence lengths seems more like
   spoken language, like a friend is talking to us. With students, discuss how
   the word choices create an emotion—nostalgia, longing—that makes the
   product appealing, even if the listeners might not ever have grilled steaks
   in their backyards at twilight to a cicada serenade. The use of imagined
   dialogue between "friends" draws us in even more.

   The words create an ideal image, maybe borrowed from movies or
   television, which connects the audience emotionally to the product being advertised, without ever mentioning a price. This is the hard part for
   the students. They are more familiar with direct persuasion, the kind that

says, "All of this for only $39.95!" To help them see the difference, have students compare ads like the beef industry ad to the ones with which they are more familiar, especially because those exclamation point–filled texts tend to be the kind students write when *they* want to be persuasive. After exploring several ads and analyzing the way writers use different varieties of language, such as how the speaker in the beef ads sometimes drops his *g*s (to sound more friendly than sophisticated), students come to see how advertisers use varieties of language—formal and informal, descriptive and commanding, personal and impersonal—to create appeal for the product in the target audience.

3. After analyzing several ads and how they use language to persuade, have students write an ad. To begin, modifying an idea by Fuchs, I have my students create a product from six items I give them: a piece of tag board, a paper clip, a rubber band, a popsicle stick, a brass fastener, and a piece of felt. They can add decorations and one other item of choice to the approved items to create their products.

4. After students have a creation, they should name it. Perrin offers ideas for teaching language through product names. Having students work through this short lesson will give them ways to use the "power of language" in naming their own products (36). When they have made the product and named it, have them write a short ad to persuade their classmates to *use* the product. I encourage them to avoid trying to "sell" the product, because then they get into cost wars, worrying about prices without paying attention to persuasive aspects of language. If students have analyzed a variety of ads effectively, they usually have several appropriate strategies they can use to write the ads for their products.

Finally, have them present their ads to the class. As they read their ads and show the product, have the class analyze the techniques of language employed and determine the effectiveness of the choices. The analysis, the writing, and the evaluation of peer ads all work to develop sensitivity to language. And the benefit to the students, as consumers who are more knowledgeable of the techniques used to entice them, will be significant.

Writing Dialogue

Although we teach students about ethos in persuasive/argument writing, Napoli asserts that, even in fiction, writers need to be believed. Some of what makes a story believable—what makes the storyteller trustworthy—is the language used by the characters. And it's hard, even for more experienced writers, to make the language of the characters sound natural, in part because of the difference between speech and writing. When students are writing creatively, they need to understand how to add credibility to their stories by creating effective dialogue.

1. According to Napoli (211–12), some of the aspects of speech that are difficult to imitate in writing are the following:

   - pitch
   - intensity
   - duration of sounds
   - the way individuals pronounce the same word differently
   - the way several people may speak at once or overlap
   - the syntax of dialects

   Help students look for how writers represent these aspects effectively by identifying and analyzing a variety of texts.

   As an example, reading aloud the beginning pages of *The Great Gatsby* (Fitzgerald) allows students to hear a particular kind of speech—more formal than today's speech, perhaps, but still more like a variety of spoken language than written. That specific speech-like quality is partly a function of word choice (*rather*, *indeed*), punctuation (lots of dashes and commas), and syntax (lots of appositives and long sentences): "It was on that slender riotous island which extends itself due east of New York—and where there are, among other natural curiosities, two unusual formations of land" (10). As students read texts, help them notice the characteristics of written language that translate into sounds for oral language. Another example book—a picture book that helps students develop a sense of how oral language can be represented in print—is *Kibitzers and Fools* (Taback). In one of the stories in the book, we can hear the American Jewish intonations:

   > "So … I'm here!" said the waiter.
   > "Taste this soup!" said the customer.
   > "Twenty-five years we have been making chicken soup," answered the waiter.
   > "Nobody has ever complained—"

   Students can see that punctuation (ellipses for pauses and exclamation points for emphasis) as well as syntax (putting "Twenty-five years" first instead of last) help to create the sound of real voices on paper. As students study novels and stories to see how the authors they read use spelling and punctuation to help readers "hear" the voices on the page, they will gain more ideas for writing their own dialogue—and deepen their awareness of the diverse ways individuals use language all around them every day.

2. Next, students need to have conversations they can practice translating into written texts. Taping conversations might create legal problems, so simply have students pay attention to conversations around them in public places and then jot down snippets of what they hear to work with more carefully in class. Chris Crowe told me that, in his preparation for writing *Mississippi Trial, 1955*, he visited the South. Then he would write down some of the phrases and sentences he heard, trying to replicate the sounds and rhythms of speech that would be true to the place.

   Because students can't travel, using movie clips or soundtracks online can allow them to hear different patterns of speech they might be able to use for characters. Have them listen to clips of actors from old movies and hear the slow drawl of John Wayne; or the more formal, crisp speech of Vincent Price; or the lilting speech of Cary Grant. Then have students compare them with clips of more current speech patterns of actors like Hugh Jackman or John Krasinski to see other speech qualities they can try to replicate in writing. Paying attention to the ways different speakers speak develops students' awareness of language.

3. As a class, practice how to replicate some of those different qualities to develop that awareness further—and also develop students' understanding of how written and oral language differ and how written language can be used to (partially) represent speech. Have students play around with using punctuation (e.g., ellipsis to show pauses) or spelling (repeating letters to show duration of sounds, as in *Wha-a-a-at?*). Have them "hear" the difference between *Pleeeeease* and *Puh-lease*. Napoli also suggests using italics or "a dash between words" to indicate stress (212–13). After practicing as a class, have students practice individually to create "voices" that they can have peers read and identify.

4. Also, teach students about using dialogue tags to overcome some of the challenges of creating effective voices in written text. Many students (at least among my classes) depend so heavily on the tags or misuse them that they diminish the credibility of the writer rather than aid in revealing the characters in the story. Napoli encourages writers to use tags that reveal the "intensity of the overall utterance," using words such as *yell*, *whisper*, *murmur*, and so on (214). She rejects using tags that don't give information about intonation (such as *giggled*, which is an act that occurs usually before or after the comment). Tags that give information evident from the text

(*asked, repeated, replied*) aren't useful. Giving student some hints about these overall intonation cues can help them write dialogue more effectively.

Rhetorical Grammar

Using Sentence Structures to Reflect Meaning

Reading aloud helps students learn about the ways sentence structures contribute to meaning—and music can help students understand rhythms of sentences.

1. When introducing students to the 1920s as a background to *The Great Gatsby* (Fitzgerald), include music of the era—namely, jazz. Students need to hear some jazz, particularly if they are unfamiliar with it. *Jazz: My Music, My People* (Monceaux) can provide background information to this listening activity, as it introduces the artists whose music influenced the time period for the novel. Be sure to have students listen to music by Duke Ellington as part of this sensory introduction so that the writing that follows will connect.

2. When students have some experience with jazz, read aloud *Duke Ellington* (Pinkney). This book provides interesting information at the same time as it allows you to teach about how the technical aspects of language—specifically, sentence structure and its effect on rhythm—can enhance our reading experience. After reading, ask students what they notice about the sound of the language. Because the book is carefully crafted so that the rhythm of the sentences sounds like jazz, students should recognize the musical element. When they do, show them some selected sentences, such as those I've included below, to indicate how Pinkney created the sound through the use of punctuation. Early in the book, we don't hear the jazzy element because Duke was encouraged to play traditional piano by his parents:

   > But his piano playing wasn't always as breezy as his stride. When Duke's mother, Daisy, and his father, J. E., enrolled him in piano lessons, Duke didn't want to go. Baseball was Duke's idea of fun. But his parents had other notions for their child.

   Contrast that rhythm with later in the book when we hear the jazz in full swing.

Yeah, those solos were kickin! Hot-buttered bop, with lots of sassy-cool tunes. When the band did their thing, the Cotton Club performers danced the Black Bottom, the Fish-Tail, and the Suzy Q.

Although word choice plays a part in the rhythm (something students should notice), they should also see that the sentences vary greatly in length, lending themselves to the rhythm that is reminiscent of the jazz music they have been listening to.

3. Be sure to consider with students why these choices might have been made. In fact, contrasting the book *Duke Ellington* with the page about him in *Jazz: My Music, My People* (Monceaux) will encourage students to see the difference. The writing by Monceaux is lovely but it isn't jazzy: "Growling, muted brass instruments, liquid clarinets, and smooth saxophones all had a place in his band, and were blended together with skill and subtlety. He used his piano to drive the rhythm of the piece and provide harmonies" (27). Have students compare the different rhythms and determine how they are created to understand how sentence structure contributes to fluency.

4. Next, have students apply this concept to their own writing by choosing to write about a topic and matching the sentence lengths and rhythm to the subject—long and slow to write about a drive through the country or walk in the park (for example), or quick and jumpy to describe the last minutes of a riveting basketball game or a wild ride at the amusement park. If students still need examples of sentences and rhythm, have them find text passages or picture books that use sentence rhythms effectively and imitate them. One book they could use is *Come on, Rain!* (Hesse). Students can contrast the heavy, slow sentences that portray the hot weather before the rain with the faster (relieved!) sentences that appear after the refreshing rain comes.

Alternative Suggestion: Students may have questions about the sentences Pinkney uses that are not traditional, complete sentences. As I mention in Chapter 3, teachers should be prepared to address the issue of "minor sentences" (Weaver, *Teaching Grammar* 252) as a stylistic choice that creates an effect. Too many writers use fragments effectively for us to tell students that they are always wrong (Schuster). Fragments or minor sentences might be inappropriate in some genres, or ineffective, or not serve a rhetorical purpose, but fragments aren't simply an issue of right and wrong. I agree with Schuster, who urges that "we must not forever exclude this writerly choice from students' revision tool kits" ("A Fresh Look" 83).

Growing Sentences

In the *Writing Next* report, Graham and Perin conclude that eleven practices are effective in helping students improve writing. One of those is *sentence combining*; in fact, they explain that sentence combining can "provide an effective alternative to traditional grammar instruction, as this approach improves students' writing quality while at the same time enhancing syntactic skills" (21). The point of sentence combining is not about making long sentences; it's about making effective sentences. It's about seeing relationships among the ideas in a sentence and considering how we want to best represent those relationships. Sentence combining is an activity that encourages students to combine ideas in a variety of ways, through one of two methods: open-ended or cued.

Open-ended combining asks students to use any method they can to combine kernel sentences into longer, more syntactically complex sentences. The advantage of the method is that students can use many options in how they combine the ideas; the disadvantage is that students are often limited to the options they know. *Cued* combining, conversely, is designed to give students clues so that they can combine sentences into certain constructions. The advantage is that students can be directed to build constructions they wouldn't ordinarily construct; the disadvantage is that the cues constrain (to a certain degree) the options available, which is not true of real writing. That is, when we write, we don't have cues directing us to combine our sentences in certain ways. On the other hand, once I learn about creating participial phrases or absolutes through cued sentence combining, I might then use them when writing my own sentences.

1. Begin by using open-ended combining, giving students sets of kernel sentences and asking them to combine them *in more than one way*. This is important. If they combine them only one way, they don't learn that sentences are flexible—and they might get the false idea that this is a right-and-wrong kind of activity. That is not what they should learn from sentence combining. After they've written different versions, have them place a star beside the one they like best. Then have students share their favorites aloud and discuss the reasons they like some sentences better than others. We also look at the original sentence—*but not to see if students match it*. Instead, we continue the discussion, theorizing why the author chose the construction they did. Discussion of the sentences and the reasons why some constructions are favored is essential for students to gain the benefits that can accrue from work with sentence combining. These discussions develop students' sensitivity to sentences and how sentence constructions can enhance meaning. These discussions also enlarge students' understanding of rhetorical effectiveness. When students are sensitive to the rhetorical effect of sentences, when they understand why some constructions appeal more than others or why some are better suited than others, they are really on the road to becoming effective writers.

2. As students continue to combine sentences, they need to have new options that extend their existing repertoires. This is a time when a teacher can introduce sentence imitation or cued sentence combining, employing sentences for these activities that use constructions students are not currently using regularly. Use the same procedures with cued combining as with open-ended. Have students combine sentences in more than one way, mark a star by the one they like best, and discuss the reason for their choices with others. The practice with cued combining, alternating with opportunities for open-ended combining, allows students to build syntactic awareness and skill. Students may not be able to name the structures they are constructing, but they can use them in their writing beyond the

practice with sentences they do in the class, especially if teachers encourage such use by expecting the constructions in polished writing the students do at other times.

Open-ended sentences can be found in a number of sources, but I prefer to make my own out of sentences my students will find in class materials. I take a sentence I think has an interesting construction that my students can practice or learn, and I break it down into its kernel sentence. I deconstruct or "de-combine" it. Sometimes I have students do this, too, so that they begin to see how many ideas can be embedded in a sentence—and sometimes they do a better job of de-combining that I do. The following are two of the sentence sets I have used with my students, taken from *An Interview with Harry the Tarantula* (Tyson):

I looked up out of the bottle.
I looked up when she opened the lid.
I looked up with my eight eyes.
I saw a huge face.
The face was staring right at me.

Original: When she opened the lid, I looked up out of the bottle with my eight eyes and saw a huge face staring right at me.

I can paralyze a cricket.
I can do it in one bite.
The poison will turn the cricket into something.
It will turn it into a morsel.
The morsel is very juicy.

Original: In one bite I can paralyze a cricket, and the poison will turn it into a very juicy morsel.

For cued sentence combining, I use some examples from books, but I have also created my own as needed. Examples of cued combining follow. The directions are to eliminate the words in italics and use the cues in parentheses to combine. The following cued set comes from *The Pearl* (Steinbeck):

The ants were busy.
They were *on the ground*. (,)
There were *big ones*.
The big ones were *black*.
The big ones had *shiny bodies*. (WITH) (,)
And there were *little ants*.
The little ones were *dusty*.
The little ones were *quick*.

Original: The ants were busy on the ground, big black ones with shiny bodies, and little dusty quick ants. (3)

Students are more likely to create specific constructions through this method than they are with open-ended combining. If they don't already have the desired constructions in their sentence repertoire, they will gain new ways of writing from this approach. After working over a period of time with both kinds of sentence combining and being expected to apply the learning to their writing, students' writing does improve its syntactic effectiveness.

Using Mentor Sentences

Imitation has a long tradition in writing instruction. I suggest it here as a method that helps students to consider language in ways that benefit them as writers. With this long tradition, it will be obvious that I am not the only person to recommend the methods that follow. Many educators today—including Ray, Anderson, Ehrenworth and Vinton, Marchetti and O'Dell, and Angelillo—advocate imitation of mentor texts as a way for students to gain understanding about language that improves their effectiveness as writers.

1. Introduce the concept of imitation by sharing good writing with students and asking them to notice sentences that stand out. When they do, ask them why they are drawn to particular sentences. When I use mentor texts with the whole class, I have ideas of particular sentences that I hope they will see, but I try to let the experience be one that allows students to explore language, finding structures that fit their needs and appeal to them as writers. To that end, students need to know how to look for sentences and structures, so we practice in class and then they work on their own. I pull sentences from the text of *Scarecrow* (Rylant), an effective test to use for imitation. The first few pages of the book contain these sentences:

   His hat is borrowed, his suit is borrowed, his hands are borrowed, even his head is borrowed.

   And his eyes probably came out of someone's drawer.

   But a scarecrow's life is all his own.

   By reading the text a few times and then looking at the way the sentences are structured, students notice many things (even from these beginning lines) that they can use in their own writing. They don't know the "names" for what they observe, but they identify the repetition of ending elements (*epistrophe*) and the use of a different phrasing to emphasize an idea. They don't always notice the lack of conjunctions in the first series of joined clauses (*asyndeton*), but sometimes they do. In later sentences in the book, they will notice the repetition of initial words (*anaphora*), the elimination of that initial repetition (*ellipsis*), and lists. After students find structures that they like, discuss the effects of the different structures. It's important that this isn't seen as just "find and copy." Discussion of the effect of the choice is essential to students' growth as writers.

2. When students understand how the structures work and what they do for the writing, have them find places in their own writing where they can experiment with those structures. Growth as writers doesn't happen all at once, but eventually, students' sensitivity to language manifests itself in their writing as they implement the structures they've imitated from published writers who use language in interesting ways.

Alternative Suggestion: Imitation can extend beyond the sentence level, too, as students develop their abilities to recognize, consider, and use textual structures and elements that are effective. For example, in *Mississippi Trial, 1955,* Chris Crowe uses language effectively to describe a place:

> Coffee. When I was at Gramma and Grampa's house, I woke up every morning to the smell of coffee. The nutty aroma floated up the back stairs and into my room through the transom window above my door. Once I was awake, I tried to separate the other aromas of my grandparents' house: some mornings the meaty, spicy scent of sausage came up the stairs; other days the sweet fragrance of fresh muffins. Behind those morning smells lingered the mellow scent of mildew, wood, and Ivory soap. To this day, if you dropped me blindfolded at my grandparents' home, I'd know I was there as soon as you opened the door. (9)

When we reread the passage, we can see the effective use of adjectives, as well as alliteration and specific details. Help students prepare to write a descriptive passage that imitates this one using these steps:

- Think of a place you have good memories of. Write down where it is.
- Put yourself in that place. Look around. Brainstorm all the smells you associate with the place.
- Choose the most significant smell. What is it? Write down the word, just the word. Now explain why that smell is significant. Then talk about the other important smells with this beginning: *Other times* . . . Then list the

least noticeable smells with this start: *Behind those smells* . . . Finally, end with this sentence and complete as appropriate for your place: "To this day, if I were taken blindfolded to _____, I'd know I was there as soon as I _____."

Here's the way I completed the imitation—and I share it to show how the imitation allowed me to use effective language to explore a memory that I hadn't thought about for years but is significant to me:

Cinnamon. That was first when we opened the door from the cold into Grandma's oven-warm kitchen. It blew in steamy gusts that accompanied us as we entered. After we unbundled ourselves, leaving coats and boots and hats and scarves and mittens in a pile by the door, I would notice the other smells: coffee first, then grandpa's cigars. Behind those, especially when I'd spend the night, I would notice the lemon polish and the musty smell of wet wool from our snowy boots soaking the rugs. To this day, if I were taken blindfolded to my grandparents' house, I'd know I was there as soon as I smelled cinnamon.

Questions for Reflection

1. What writing assignments do you currently give students that could be adjusted to include a component that enhances your students' language learning?

2. How can you make writing and grammar more integrated in your classroom?

3. Where in other places of the writing process, besides editing, can you include language lessons that will benefit your students as writers?

Reading and Language

Why are we reading, if not in the hope of beauty laid bare, life heightened and its deepest mysteries probed?

—*Annie Dillard* (The Writing Life)

A colleague told me a story about being on a jury. One piece of evidence—a statement by a witness—was a point of contention in the jury room. The foreman, an English teacher, used grammar (explaining subordinate clauses and their functions) to help the rest of the jury accurately interpret the statement. Knowing something about language and grammar can help us read—and understand what we read—better.

As I showed in Chapter 2, it is a valued practice to use reading (mentor texts) to teach grammar for writing. But this chapter, focusing on the language in the NCTE/IRA Standards for the English Language Arts, centers on teaching grammar as a way to help students develop as readers and language users.

We have all read and heard a lot of advice about using grammar to teach writing, but not as much about reading and grammar. Eileen Simmons makes this point in the introduction to an *English Journal* article where she realizes that her students were having trouble comprehending their reading of *The Odyssey* because they didn't understand grammar: "There was no way I could deny what students—through their work—were telling me. They needed grammar to improve their reading comprehension" (48). Massey asserts that grammar can mark "an important point of contact between form and content, as, as such, it also constitutes a powerful analytical lens for textual (i.e., literary/rhetorical) analysis and criticism, which remains a bedrock of an integrated language arts curriculum" (66). Doniger clearly agrees when he describes how he uses grammar—"inverted word order and unexpected word usage," as well as "apposition, hyperbole, and redundancy"—to aid students in their comprehension of Shakespeare's plays (8).

Benjamin also uses grammar to help students become more effective readers. Although she uses grammar terms in her teaching of literature, she doesn't worry about how well the students know those terms: "You can't wait until students come to you already knowing what it is you wish to teach them. Just start talking. Infuse the basics along with some more sophisticated concepts" (3). Some teachers might worry that students won't "get" what the lesson is if they don't know terms first. My experience is that students have enough general knowledge of language to understand the gist of the concepts, and they will learn what they need. The key is that the object here is to teach literature with grammar, not to teach grammar through literature. Benjamin summarizes her approach as using "grammar as a flashlight to illuminate literature" (5). I like that simile. It reminds me to keep the focus on the literature, not grammar terms.

So, what might this look like? Let's look into a classroom reading *Al Capone Does My Shirts* (Choldenko). The class is in the middle of reading Chapter 11; we pause with this passage:

> At UCLA they made us cut Natalie's hair. Shaved it right off. They tested her like she was some kind of insect. They tested the movement of her eyes, the sensitivity of her ears, the color of her pee. They tested allergies, reflexes, muscle strength. Her speech in a dark room. Her reaction to Tchaikovsky. The way she ate, slept, burped, blew her nose and even what she thought. Especially what she thought. Nothing about her was private.

TEACHER: Let's pause here. What was happening to Natalie at UCLA?

SKYLER: She was getting tested. Tested to see what was wrong.

MARYGRACE: Yeah. They wanted to know if she had something they could treat.

TEACHER: Okay. Why were they allowed?

SEAN: Her mom wanted answers. She wanted someone to make Natalie better.

EMILY: But her mom was kind of blind. I mean, really, she just lives for one solution after another, right? Isn't that what it just said?

TEACHER: What does Moose think about it?

JOY: He sounds kind of mad about it.

HARRISON: Definitely. He seems upset.

TEACHER: How do you know? Does he say he's mad? No? So how do we know he's upset by the testing?

SEAN: He says it was like an insect. That sounds bad, like not human.

TEACHER (*after a pause*): Okay. Anything else you see to get at that feeling?

BRITNEY (*after a pause*): It's kind of the way he says it, like all the things piled on top of each other. That makes it sound upset.

SARA: Yeah. And also some kind of short sentences—like the kind we say when we're mad: "Stop, I mean it. Cut it out." It sounds all choppy like that. Mad.

BRETT: But there are some long sentences in there, too. That one close to the end is kind of long.

TEACHER: Anything else you notice? (*Nothing.*) Well, those are some interesting things where the author uses the structure of sentences to convey meaning without saying it. All those stacks of words? That's an old rhetorical device from ancient Greece called *asyndeton* that is a list without a conjunction (like *and*) before the last word.

SEAN: Wait?! Do we have to know that word?

TEACHER: No. Don't worry. It won't be on a quiz or anything. I just want you to see how a writer might use something that's been around for a long time. It's stuck around because it's a really useful tool. In this case, it helps us see how Moose is feeling—upset because they were doing too much that seemed invasive to him. But think about how we might use the same tool in our daily lives. Can you think of any times it might be useful? Start with how it makes us feel.

JILL: Kind of overwhelmed.

JAMES: Crowded in, like lots of stuff shoved at me without a chance to think.

JILL: Yeah, I like that.

TEACHER: Might we ever want to create that effect in our writing or talk? Can you think of an example?

TEACHER (*after a pause*): Okay, well, just keep thinking. Let's just touch on the other device you notice about sentence length. Some of these "sentences" aren't really sentences, are they? "Her speech in a dark room," for example. We know that isn't a sentence because there is no action in the group of words. What do we call a group of words that is not a sentence but it's punctuated like a sentence? Does anyone know?

MARK: It's a fragment. I kept getting marked for that last year in my writing. (*Some chuckling.*)

TEACHER: Well, you are absolutely right. They are called *fragments*, and they are useful in some places in some kinds of writing, but maybe not all the time or in all kinds of writing. What is the effect they create here?

MARK: Here it seems like a longer piece of the list. Just broken off.

TEACHER: I like that. It is like it's broken off from another sentence. Why break it off?

JAMIE: Well, it's kind of like all those last bits—fragments, I guess—could start with "They tested," right? "They tested allergies, reflexes, muscle strength." *They tested* "her speech in a dark room." *They tested* "her reaction to Tchaikovsky." *They tested* "the way she ate, slept, burped, blew her nose and even what she thought."

JILL: Yeah. That makes sense. So the author was just cutting off the ends?

SUSAN: Maybe she didn't want to repeat the *they tested* parts?

TEACHER: Maybe. Why wouldn't she want to repeat the sentence beginnings?

MARK: Hey! I got marked off for that, too, last year!

SHAY: My teacher last year told us to start our sentences with different words, so that's probably why she didn't want to repeat, even though that's what she meant.

TEACHER: Well, there are times we want to be careful with sentence beginnings—we don't want to bore our readers—but sometimes . . . remember how we talked about how sometimes the rules are to warn us but don't have to stop us? I'm thinking that there might be a different reason here.

Remember Sara's comment earlier, about how choppy this feels, broken up? Could that be a consideration?

SARA: That's what I was thinking earlier. I was thinking that it felt choppy, like how we feel when we are upset.

TEACHER: I want you all to hold onto that idea for a minute. Let's read a little further on this page and see what we feel a few paragraphs down. (*Reading, then pausing after this passage.*)

> Things fell apart at my house after that. Ants in the sink. Flies on the garbage. Cereal for supper. No clean dishes. Natalie in the same dirty dress. The blood of picked scabs on her arm.

TEACHER: Now, what do you feel here? What is Moose feeling?

SARA: It's the same! All the short sentences? Are these fragments?

TEACHER: Well, they have some nouns in them, but I don't see any verbs. Ants . . . doing what? Flies . . . doing what? Usually sentences need both parts: the doer and the action. So I would say most of these sentences are fragments. What is the feeling from using them? How do they help us know what Moose feels?

JAMES: His life is apart. And all these sentences are just parts. So the sentences kind of seem like his life, all messed up.

SKYLER: Yeah. The details—flies, ants, scabs . . . those are bad enough. But the way he says it, well, you just kind of feel bad for him. He must feel bad.

JILL: I think so, too. The choppy sentences feel like a sad life, nothing is right or normal. The sentences say it, but they are also kind of acting like it. Does that make sense?

TEACHER: It does to me. It tells me that the way this author writes about Moose can help us see beyond the words to how Moose is feeling, especially as he is a guy who doesn't really say his feelings out loud, right? Let's read on, but let's not forget that we can see inside Moose sometimes more than he lets on.

What follows are some teaching suggestions for each of the five concepts discussed in Chapter 1. Although the texts used as examples may not be ones used in your classroom, the ideas can be adapted to other texts and to a variety of grade levels.

Traditional Grammar

Grammar and Tone

I can never decide if I would rather have Halloween fall on a school day or not. The day after is often worse. There is no getting around the fact that the first major holiday after school starts has an impact on students, no matter what grade level they're in. I've tried ignoring the fact that I'm trying to teach Homer or Shakespeare to a group of fully costumed ghouls, pirates, rock stars, babies, or bunnies. Instead, I've decided to embrace the day. I found a book that I can use to address the costumes and still feel as though I'm teaching students. The book, *Halloween Pie* (Tunnell), tells the story of a witch who bakes a pie and then casts a spell on it as she leaves it to cool on her windowsill. The regular Halloween cast—a vampire, a ghoul, a ghost, a banshee, a zombie, and a skeleton— catch the scent and eat the pie. What happens to them lets readers know what the spell is. It's a fun story, and it uses a lot of grammatical elements to make it work. So, as a class, we talk about grammar in the context of the book, particularly how the story is enhanced by the grammar.

One thing I like about using *Halloween Pie*—or any picture book—is that students often have the mistaken belief that picture books are easy to write, that they aren't necessarily crafted with the same skill that longer stories or books are. Although the language is more accessible than that of Dickens or Shakespeare, perhaps, the authors of picture books use just as much care to craft effective texts as other authors do—if not more. Although our discussion doesn't necessarily help students access difficult content, it does help them understand the care with language that all authors take to enhance the tone or message of their writing.

1. Begin by reading the story aloud—and showing the pictures—so that students know the plot. Then, go back to specific parts to explore the story through grammar. For instance, when the creatures get to the witch's house, they all yell for the pie: "Give me some pie!" But the dialogue tags are different: "called," "bawled," "sighed," "cried," "groaned," and "moaned." The verbs rhyme, but they also match the speaker (ghoul, banshee, and so forth). Discuss the author's choice to have each speaker say the same line: Is six times too many? Why or why not? How do the different tags help individualize the characters, especially when the dialogue is the same?

2. Eventually, the spell begins to take effect, and all the pie eaters fall asleep. Tunnell uses a series of six short sentences to describe this development,

but each sentence uses a different verb and a different prepositional phrase to indicate where the creature slept: "fell asleep before the fire," "dreamed in an empty drawer," "dozed behind the door." Discuss the author's choices in using sentences of the same length and parallel structure but varying the verbs used for the same action. Have students try to rewrite this section and see if combining the ideas is more or less effective. Focus the discussion on how the author's choices enhance a story in a picture book but might not be effective in other kinds of writing, such as a webpage or op-ed.

3. Later, when the witch returns home and finds the pie gone, she discovers something else instead: "Loafing before the fire was a perfectly shaped pumpkin. . . . Scattered inside the drawer was a smidgeon of salt. Swinging from the rafters was a sack of sweet sugar." All the ingredients the witch needs to make a new pie—and all where the creatures had fallen asleep. After I tell students that the structures that begin the sentences are part of the verb phrase, we look at the sentence patterns. It's clear that the subject of the sentence is the last word or last part of the sentence. We talk about how we normally would say the sentences: "A perfectly shaped pumpkin was loafing before the fire," for example. Why did the author choose to rearrange the order? What is the effect? Students notice that the inverted order requires me to slow the reading down, thus focusing on plot and giving students a chance to make connections, because we didn't know what spell the witch had cast. Other students notice that the word order emphasizes where the ingredients are, linking the locations to the characters that had fallen asleep in those places. Sentence structure helps tie the sections of the story together, making it clearer for the reader.

Alternative Suggestion: If you don't have access to *Halloween Pie*, use another picture book that uses parts of speech and sentence structure to affect meaning, such as *Dear Fish* (Gall). In that book, most pages have a series of four words—verbs or nouns, although many of the nouns are gerunds—that add detail to the story. Read the story without the repetition of the rhyming nouns and verbs, and then read it again with them included so that students see how those words add detail and depth to the story. Students might consider how the repetition of different parts of speech creates different tones.

This way of using discussion about parts of speech to look at textual effects could also be used with traditional (not picture) books. For example, the first few chapters of *A Tale of Two Cities* (Dickens) lend themselves to a discussion of how grammar enhances meaning. In the second chapter, for instance, the repeated use of conjunctions creates an interesting effect:

> He walked uphill in the mire by the side of the mail, as the rest of the passengers did; not because they had the least relish for walking exercise, under the circumstances, but because the hill, and the harness, and the mud, and the mail, were all so heavy, that the horse had three times already come to a stop, besides once drawing the coach across the road, with the mutinous intent of taking it back to Blackheath. (15–16)

Whew! Don't we feel as tired as the passenger did? Did we forget that this sentence was initially about that one man? The repeated use of conjunctions slows the passage down; add in commas, prepositional phrases, and unusual word order, and the whole sentence begins to feel as if it, too, were climbing a hill through mud.

Thus, investigating grammar can help students comprehend their reading in ways that don't necessarily require them to know the terms of the structures they explore. Although I think this idea can be applied to almost any text, many of the historical texts we read with students benefit from this application of grammar: *Wuthering Heights* (Brontë), *Pride and Prejudice* (Austen), *Great Expectations* (Dickens).

Grammar and Description

Benjamin's example of using traditional grammar to help students better understand a text provides a good model. Her process is as follows:

- She introduces *The Grapes of Wrath* (Steinbeck) by giving students a copy of the first paragraph—without modifiers. Students discuss the language and the mood that is being established.

- Then she shows them the same paragraph with adjectives and adverbs, to help them feel "Steinbeck's use of color and texture" (4).

- Finally, she gives them the complete first paragraph with prepositional phrases added. "At this point, the text blossoms for us with its full intended effect, an effect so much more powerful because we withheld the detail" (4).

Benjamin's process can work with different texts. For example, the beginning of *Where the Red Fern Grows* (Rawls) describes a dogfight in language that contains a lot of participles—more than are found in other parts of the chapters. There's a reason for that, and students who explore it can come to understand how this particular grammatical construction adds to the meaning of the passage.

1. First have students read the following passage that has the participles removed:

    I was trying to make up my mind to help when I got a surprise. Up out of that mass reared an old redbone hound. For a second I saw him. I caught my breath. I couldn't believe what I had seen.

    He fought his way through the pack and backed up under the low branches of a hedge. They formed a halfmoon circle around him. A big bird dog, bolder than the others, darted in. The hedge shook as he tangled with the hound. He came out so fast he fell over backwards. I saw that his right ear was split wide open. It was too much for him and he took off down the street.

    A big ugly cur tried his luck. He didn't get off so easy. He came out with his left shoulder laid open to the bone. He sat down on his rear and let the world know that he had been hurt.

    By this time, my blood was boiling. It's hard for a man to stand and watch an old hound fight against such odds, especially if that man has memories in his heart like I had in mine. I had seen the time when an old hound like that had given his life so that I might live.

    I waded in. My yelling and scolding didn't have much effect, but the coat did. The dogs scattered and left. (Rawls 2, with parts deleted)

2. Ask students what they can hear and see in the passage. Most of the time, they have some answers; often, though, they'll have questions. After they share their responses, have students read the original passage, included below with participles and participial phrases italicized:

    I was trying to make up my mind to help when I got a surprise. Up out of that *snarling, growling, slashing* mass reared an old redbone hound. For a second I saw him. I caught my breath. I couldn't believe what I had seen.

    Twisting and slashing, he fought his way through the pack and backed up under the low branches of a hedge. *Growling and snarling*, they formed a half-moon circle around him. A big bird dog, bolder than the others, darted in. The hedge shook as he tangled with the hound. He came out so fast he fell over backwards. I saw that his right ear was split wide open. It was too much for him and he took off down the street, *squalling like a scalded cat*.

A big ugly cur tried his luck. He didn't get off so easy. He came out with his left shoulder laid open to the bone. He sat down on his rear and let the world know that he had been hurt.

By this time, my *fighting* blood was boiling. It's hard for a man to stand and watch an old hound fight against such odds, especially if that man has memories in his heart like I had in mine. I had seen the time when an old hound like that had given his life so that I might live.

Taking off my coat, I waded in. My yelling and scolding didn't have much effect, but the *swinging* coat did. The dogs scattered and left. (Rawls 2, with parts deleted)

3. Now ask students the same question again: What can they see and hear? They'll have more to say now! They should notice that, along with adding sensory details, the participles—those *-ing* words that were deleted in the first version—actually intensify the ferocity of the fight. The words themselves, their meanings and their sounds, help to create the action in and movement of the fight: "twisting and slashing," "growling and snarling."

4. To help students understand what Noden explains about participles, that they "evoke action" and that "using single participles creates rapid movement, while expanded phrases add details at a slower, but equally intense pace" (4–5), have them consider the effects of the shorter or longer participles. For example, look at the participial phrase that ends the second paragraph—"squalling like a scalded cat." What is the effect if we say only *scalded*? It's faster. Have students add details to the other participles and then consider the effect: "Twisting *his red body* and slashing *at the dogs with his paws*, he fought his way through the pack. . . . Growling *deep in their throats* and snarling *through their teeth*, they formed a halfmoon circle around him." The effect is very different. Slower. Not as tight or quick as the scene that's written in the book—or, perhaps, the scene Rawls wanted us to picture.

5. Have students read the rest of the first chapter, looking for participles and participial phrases. Students should notice that there aren't very many. Have them speculate why that might be. They should see that participles, especially the one-word kind, aren't as necessary in this chapter for the ideas that have to do with healing and that show a slower, less intense pace. When students approach the end of the book, help them review this lesson by looking again for participles in the scene where the narrator and his dogs are attacked by a mountain lion. In that passage (Rawls 225–28),

many participles and participial phrases are used to show action and create intensity.

6. In their enthusiasm, students sometimes confuse verbs that end in *-ing* with participles. That is something teachers should anticipate and is a distinction they should be ready to clarify. Although the two look alike, when the word is the action, it's a verb; when it's describing the actor, it's a participle. Students also sometimes notice that some verbs ending in *-ing* act like nouns, as "yelling" and "scolding" in the next to the last sentence. Those are gerunds. Although students may not care to know the name, it's a good idea to be prepared in case they identify them in their search.

Alternative Suggestion: This plan can be applied to any text that uses participles in the same way—to represent action or to create intensity. In the near final scene of *Lord of the Flies* (Golding), before the boys are rescued, Ralph is running from the fire and the "savage" (184). That passage is full of participles and participial phrases that create an intense feeling of panic. In another text, *Mississippi Trial, 1955* (Crowe), longer participial phrases create intensity of emotion: "I wrapped my arms around Grampa's neck and hugged him while we cried together, mourning the loss of a wife and grandmother and friend, wondering how we could possible survive without her" (28). Students could rewrite the passage as three sentences, noticing the effect the use of the participial phrases creates in that significant moment. As we spot these structures in our reading, we can help students see how they are useful to understand the text and the language that creates emotion for readers.

Teachers can apply this process to any element of grammar that contributes significantly to the meaning. In *Mississippi Trial, 1955*, Crowe makes effective use of adjectives to set scenes:

> Ralph and Ronnie Remington even came over to pay their respects. Ronnie wore a black suit coat stretched to button across his wide belly; a limp bow tie hung cockeyed from the collar of his white shirt. Ralph wore a blue tuxedo jacket with navy blue pants, shiny at the knees. He carried a champagne bottle with a wide purple bow tied around its neck. Both men looked about as comfortable as cows in a slaughterhouse. (29)

Using a process modeled after Benjamin's, prepare copies of the text without the adjectives so that students can recognize how grammatical elements contribute to the mood and message of a text. Other books with passages that make use of specific verbs or unique adjectives to set a mood include *A Separate Peace* (Knowles 4–6, 22–23) and *Lord of the Flies* (Golding 7–8, 134–35).

Editing

Punctuation and Pausing

In *Eats, Shoots and Leaves: The Zero Tolerance Approach to Punctuation*, Truss establishes a base for explaining how punctuation can affect meaning: "On the page, punctuation performs its grammatical function, but in the mind of the reader it does more than that. It tells the reader how to hum the tune" (71). When students hear passages with effective punctuation read aloud, they gain a sense of how punctuation matters, how it helps create meaning.

1. In *My Ántonia* (Cather), the punctuation is especially effective when reading aloud. In the following passage, Cather uses commas to good effect, but she also makes use of dashes, semicolons, and colons to create pauses of different lengths and intensity. Begin by having students close their eyes and listen as you read aloud the passage. Then have students follow along in the text as you read aloud the passage again.

   > When spring came, after that hard winter, one could not get enough of the nimble air. Every morning I wakened with a fresh consciousness that winter was over. There were none of the signs of spring for which I used to watch in Virginia, no budding woods or blooming gardens. There was only—spring itself; the throb of it, the light restlessness, the vital essence of it everywhere: in the sky, in the swift clouds, in the pale sunshine, and in the warm, high wind—rising suddenly, sinking suddenly, impulsive and playful like a big puppy that pawed you and then lay down to be petted. If I had been tossed down blindfold on that red prairie, I should have known that it was spring. (119–20)

2. During a third read-aloud, ask students to measure which marks of punctuation create the longest or most emphatic pauses—down to those that create the softest or shortest of the ones used in this passage. Then have students get into small groups to discuss their findings (they often disagree about them). Have them relate their findings to the effects the different pauses create in the text. How do longer pauses focus attention on what the writer wants the reader to focus on? How do softer pauses allow for decreased focus? After their work in groups, have students bring their ideas to a whole-class discussion. Even if students don't agree on their findings, such a discussion helps students understand how punctuation marks matter to a piece of writing, how they contribute to meaning.

Alternative Suggestion: Any passage in a text that uses varying kinds of punctuation can be used in the same way to raise students' awareness of the connection between punctuation and reading and meaning. This is especially true of poetry, including poems by Emily Dickinson and Robert Frost. Another way to consider this concept would be with visual texts such as infographics where students can consider how font style and size work in similar ways to punctuation in terms of directing readers' attention and focus.

Punctuation and Meaning

Another way to look at punctuation's influence on meaning is by analyzing how a writer uses a particular point of punctuation. I use an approach similar to the one suggested by Petit but with "A Modest Proposal" (Swift).

1. Make sure that students begin with an understanding of satire and irony before reading the essay. After reading it, have students explore Swift's intent and meaning though discussion, possibly addressing some of the following questions, among others:

   - How does Swift establish his credibility in the essay? Why is it important that he do so?
   - What kind of evidence does Swift use to support his assertions? Why are those types of evidence useful to him?
   - Where is the evidence that Swift is being satirical and not serious?

   It's important to help students understand the text (this or any other used in this application) before moving on to an analysis of the use of punctuation in

---

Extending Your Knowledge

Lance Massey notes that:

> Far from merely being a superficial feature of writing—a formal adornment draped over some deeper substance known as "content," or perhaps a rigid mold into which substantive content is poured—grammar can and does play an important role in the construction of textual meaning. After all, grammatical choices can affect levels of formality, amplify poetic language and meaning, and even reflect deep epistemological orientations. (66)

Many students (and even some teachers) think of punctuation as right or wrong, there or not, when it is often much more than that and can contribute to meaning. Helping students learn that can change them as readers.

helping to create meaning—because the point isn't so much the use of punctuation as it is its effect on the content.

2. Have students work in small groups to identify sentences in the essay that use semicolons. Then ask students to cluster the sentences they found into pairs or groups that use semicolons in the same way or for similar purposes, as shown in the following examples:

> The question therefore is how this number shall be reared and provided for; which, as I have already said, under the present situation of affairs, is utterly impossible by all the methods hitherto proposed. (Swift 802)

> But as to myself, having been wearied out for many years with offering vain, idle, visionary thought, and at length utterly despairing of success, I fortunately fell upon this proposal; which, as it is wholly new, so it hath something solid and real, of no expense and little trouble, full in our own power, and whereby we can incur no danger in disobliging English. (808)

Or as in this pair:

> Some persons of a desponding spirit are in great concern about the vast number of poor people who are aged, diseased, or maimed; and I have been desired to employ my thoughts what course may be taken to ease the nation of so grievous an encumbrance. (805)

> And as to the younger laborers, they are now in almost as hopeful a condition: they cannot get work and consequently pine away for want of nourishment to a degree that if at any time they are accidentally hired to common labor, they have not strength to perform it; and thus the country and themselves are in a fair way of being soon delivered from the evils to come. (806)

Or this set:

> For we can neither employ them in handicraft or agriculture; we neither build houses (I mean in the country) nor cultivate land. (802)

> Thus the squire will learn to be a good landlord and grow popular among his ten-

ants; the mother will have eight shillings net profit and be fit for work until she produces another child. (804)

Students should be able to find several more examples for these patterns and at least one more pattern of semicolon use in the essay. When students have made the groups of sentences, have them give a name to the way the semicolon is used to combine ideas in each grouping. For instance, for the first pair I show, they might call it the "'which' combination." Students may develop different names for groups of sentences, and that's okay. Naming the groups is not an activity meant to measure correctness; it is simply a way for students to notice and label what they've found in order to compare it more effectively with other constructions.

3. Next, have students look for *nonexamples*. That is, have them find sentences with the same structure that do *not* use the semicolon. So, for the first pair, I give students the following sentence: "I shall now therefore humbly propose my own thought, which I hope will not be liable to the least objection" (Swift 803). Students note that this sentence, like the ones in the set I identified, has a first "part," followed by a second "part" that begins with "which"; they will probably not identify the parts as clauses, which is okay. We just want them to see parallels so that they can now compare the examples with the nonexamples and begin to generalize about the reason for the semicolon's use when it is used. For example, students might decide that the use of the semicolon in the "'which' combination" actually makes the reader pay more attention to the two separate ideas than they would in the nonexample. The semicolon creates a more noticeable pause between the two parts; if a person were reading the sentences aloud (a good suggestion for this analysis), the voice tends to drop more, as it would for sentence-ending punctuation rather than the slighter pause necessitated by the more common comma. Thus, we read the two parts with more emphasis on each part. Students should consider why Swift would want that emphasis in the examples and not in the nonexamples. As they do so, their insight on the satire and meaning of the essay increases.

Extending Your Knowledge

Bonnie Warne says that "punctuation imitates what our voices do when we speak" (25). If we can help our students see that punctuation aids meaning when the speaker is absent, we can move them a long way toward understanding nuances of language.

Alternative Suggestion: This procedure can be used with any text (or parts of texts) that use punctuation in interesting ways that contribute to the text's meaning. Thoreau's *Walden and Civil Disobedience* and Stoker's *Dracula* are two such texts. But you can also use the process with other punctuation that provides insight on how a text is written (and, thus, how it carries meaning). For example, *The Woman Warrior* (Kingston) could serve as a noteworthy study of the use of dashes and the way they contribute to the tone and meaning in a text.

Teachers with whom I have shared this process have found many texts that benefit from paying attention to punctuation as a way to delve more deeply into meaning. And, when students are paying attention to punctuation in this way, even though they may not immediately apply it (although I would recommend such application—e.g., write a paragraph about the satire in Swift's essay and use semicolons at least once to create an effect as he did), they will still be developing sensitivity to aspects of language that are important to them as readers and writers.

Usage

Dialect and Emotion

In *Their Eyes Were Watching God,* Hurston uses dialect to help readers "see" characters' feelings in ways that Standard English might not allow. Such use of dialect points to limitations of Standard English rather than issues of power often associated with usage. In fact, the novel's foreword includes an account of how the novel was not accepted during the 1940s and acknowledges language as part of the reason for that lack of acceptance: "The quieter voice of a woman searching for self-realization could not, or would not, be heard" (x).

1. Prepare students for the characters' language by reading aloud at least some of the book. By listening to the language as they follow along in their texts, students can feel and hear the rhythm of the language—and see how meaning is carried in more than the words alone. Hearing the voices aloud at first helps me create the voices in my head so that later, while reading to myself, I can still hear those voices and their rhythm and usage. That's what I want to do for students, too.

2. As you read the book, notice places in the text (I'll identify two below) where the usage shifts—mid-paragraph—from more standard usage to the dialect of the characters. After students read these passages, ask them why they think the author constructed the passage the way she did.

So Janie began to think of Death. Death, that strange being with the huge square toes who lived way in the West. The great one who lived in the straight house like a platform without sides to it, and without a roof. What need has Death for a cover, and what winds can blow against him? He stands in his high house that overlooks the world. Stands watchful and motionless all day with his sword drawn back, waiting for the messenger to bid him come. Been standing there before there was a where or a when or a then. She was liable to find a feather from his wings lying in her yard any day now. She was sad and afraid too. Poor Jody! He ought not to have to wrassle in there by himself. She sent Sam to suggest a visit, but Jody said No. These medical doctors wuz all right with the Godly sick, but they didn't know a thing about a case like his. (Hurston 84)

The thing made itself into pictures and hung around Janie's bedside all night long. Anyhow, she wasn't going back to Eatonville to be laughed at and pitied. She had ten dollars in her pocket and twelve hundred in the bank. But oh God, don't let Tea Cake be off somewhere hurt and Ah not know nothing about it. And God, please suh, don't let him love nobody else but me. Maybe Ah'm is uh fool, Lawd, lak dey say, but Lawd, Ah been so lonesome, and Ah been waitin', Jesus. Ah done waited uh long time. (120)

Use questions like the following to guide discussion:

- What does it reveal to shift usage in these passages? What do these shifts represent in terms of the characters? In terms of plot? In terms of social and cultural relationships?
- What meaning might such shifts have in our own use of language?
- What does consideration of this shifting nature of language tell us about the social aspects of language, not only the language we use with others, but the language we use in our most private thoughts?

In one response to these questions, the shifts seem to suggest the inadequacy of standard usage to represent our deepest feelings or emotions. Gates interprets this shifting between vernacular and standard usage in the narrator's voice as "a verbal analogue" that represents being a "woman in a male-dominated world and . . . a black person in a nonblack world" (203).

3. Have students consider how usage connects to our emotions and to the roles we play as we move through different situations in our lives. Have students reflect on their own more obvious shifts in usage—writing a text message versus writing an essay for school, for example. These shifts also reflect roles and relationships in varying social situations. How can the same thing be true for the characters in the novel?

Randy Bomer notes that good readers hear shifts in voices, hear the way different voices sound—including the narrator's voice: "To read … without hearing a shift in voice is to lose much of the pleasure of the text and is also probably a good sign that the reader is not making meaning" (525). Helping our students learn to hear those different voices helps them improve as readers.

Alternative Suggestion: A favorite picture book of mine, *Show Way* (Woodson), works in a similar way, showing how dialect can open readers to the emotion of the characters. The rhythm of the vernacular lets us into the feelings of the women in the book: "Had herself a baby girl and named that child Mathis Way. Loved that baby up so. Yes, she loved that baby up." If this passage were written in Standard English, readers would be limited in sensing the emotion and personality communicated through the dialect.

Dialect and Character

In the picture book *The Perfect Pumpkin Pie* (Cazet), dialect helps to reveal character. From his first full sentence in the book, "I does love a perfect pie," Old Man Wilkerson reveals himself to be the ideal character to become an irascible ghost—unlike Grandma with her more standard language. These characters offer examples of different levels of formality that help to reveal character.

Strong identifies three levels of formality that can be helpful to students in discerning more about character. For each style level, he notes the voice, diction, syntax, and contexts associated with that level of formality. So, for instance, he notes that *high style* is formal and detached, and uses abstract words or words that draw attention to themselves in long sentences and fully developed paragraphs. High style is used in contexts that are usually formal or ceremonial. By contrast, the *low* (informal) *style* is chatty and rambling, using slang words and contractions in syntax that mirrors speech. This style is more appropriate for journals and emails. As different characters speak, readers are able to see different levels of formality in their language, which should encourage discussion as to what these uses of language reveal about the characters.

1. After reading the story with students, ask them to compare and contrast the levels of formality of the two main characters' language. Students should gather some key statements from each, as in the list below, and then make some determinations about how each set reveals different levels of formality (subject-verb agreement, pronoun use, vocabulary, etc.). Have

them discuss how the differing levels of formality reflect aspects of each individual character:

OLD MAN WILKERSON:

- I does love a perfect pie.
- That pie ain't perfect, there's things a-missin'.
- I knows me pumpkins, so's you better comply.

GRANDMA:

- I think everyone loves a good pumpkin pie.
- He's a ghostly fussbudget with an appetite for a good pie.
- Pumpkin pies attract nothing but trouble. (Cazet)

2. To reinforce the idea of the first part of this activity, ask students to take Old Man Wilkerson's statements and rewrite them in more formal levels of language. "That pie isn't perfect. There is something missing." What is gained and what is lost in terms of the character development if we change his language? Why might that work against the point and tone of the story?

Alternative Suggestion: Other books that show characters using different dialects or levels of formality in language can benefit from the same exploration of how language reflects character. *Cold Sassy Tree* (Burns), *A Day No Pigs Would Die* (Peck), and *Monster* (Myers) are three options. Students might consider how the different levels of language reveal character—and how the characters might be differently represented if they were assigned the same usage—formal or informal, slang or dialect. *Flossie and the Fox* (McKissack) is another picture book where the dialogue alternates between vernacular and standard dialects. Using books like these in the classroom can help students learn about the richness of the English language—in all its varieties—and how dialects help authors reflect character.

Discussions could also occur with a number of pieces of literature that show language use differing from one group to another or from one situation to another. Calpurnia changes dialects in *To Kill a Mockingbird* when she takes the children to her church—and she explains why she makes the shift: "Now what if I talked white-folks' talk at church, and with my neighbors? They'd think I was puttin' on airs to beat Moses. . . . It's not ladylike. It aggravates 'em" (Lee 126). In *The Bean Trees* (Kingsolver), when LouAnn meets Taylor, she says, "You talk just like me" (102). That observation provides an occasion to discuss the dialects of the two characters, especially what constitutes a dialect, because, in some ways, the women's speech isn't very different from informal speech found in other areas around the United States.

Sensitive Language

Sometimes objections are raised about reading novels in the classroom because of their use of painful language, including racial slurs. It is certainly something teachers need to be particularly cognizant of if they teach these novels, including frequently taught titles such as *Adventures of Huckleberry Finn* (Twain), *To Kill a Mockingbird* (Lee), *Roll of Thunder, Hear My Cry* (Taylor), or *Of Mice and Men* (Steinbeck).

Mildred Taylor, in her "Note to the Reader" in *The Land*, has this to say about her use of painful language in her novels:

> All of my books are based on stories told by my family, and on the history of the United States. In my writing I have attempted to be true to those stories and the history. I have included characters, incidents, and language that present life as it was in many parts of the United States before the Civil Rights Movement.
>
> Although there are those who wish to ban my books because I have used language that is painful, I have chosen to use the language that was spoken during the period, for I refuse to white-wash history. The language was painful and life was painful for many African Americans, including my family.
>
> I remember the pain. ("Note to the Reader")

If we teach novels that contain language that is painful—slurs, epithets, name-calling—it's important to help students understand that such language is meant not to be emulated but to add knowledge of the situation and the pain of the characters—as well as the insensitivity and thoughtlessness of others. Discussing this sensitive issue from the position of an author's choice to present difficult situations helps students see the use of such language from a more positive perspective—and not as language they would want to use themselves.

Some people recommend that these books simply not be taught. Although Borsheim-Black and Sarigianides acknowledge that, in some ways, not teaching a book because of its language results in a type of censorship, they also recognize that sometimes the books are actually required to be taught. What should a teacher do, when "a text proves so offensive to students *required* to read it and have it read *aloud*, in *mandatory*, *public* schooling, especially a term garnering such rage and humiliation for people of color, and especially in White-dominant context" (57, emphasis in original)?

Justin Grinage and Koritha Mitchell both provide recommendations for how to handle the use of racial slurs in texts in classrooms. Grinage's recommendations can apply to a variety of novels:

1. Prepare yourself and your students by giving students notice that the class will be reading a book with sensitive, possibly painful language. Grinage recommends at least a week. During that week or before, establish the expectations for class discussions about sensitive topics.

2. Write about the offensive word(s). Although Grinage's focus is specifically on a racial slur and students' feelings about it, Keely describes having her students research and write about a variety of "dangerous" words as a way to help them make "more responsible life decisions" (60). In both cases, students grapple with their own feelings about the words that are used in literature: how they make them feel, how it might feel to hear the words aloud in class, etc.

3. Using background from *Nigger: The Strange Career of a Troublesome Word* (R. Kennedy), Grinage shares some background, history, and modern usage of the offensive word students will encounter in the novels mentioned above. He also shares personal experiences about how the word has affected him and his family.

4. Set up expectations for reading aloud and discussions. It should be established that no one uses the slur as it is written in the book. Grinage recommends using "the N-word" in its place. The same practice might be used with other words modern texts might use that demean other groups represented in our classes.

5. Encourage students to reflect after reading the novel to see if their views on some of the hurtful terms have changed.

Language Change

Names and Naming

In *Romeo and Juliet* (Shakespeare), Juliet suggests that names don't change identity in her famous line "A rose by any other name would smell as sweet" (2.2.43–44). However, most of us know that naming is a serious action—and we are aware that the names people use to label others for good or ill often stick. Sometimes those names are words that have been around for a long time but are now being used in new ways (*pimp* and *gay* are two examples), but the use of names carries emotional baggage. Considering names and their associations with them can help students understand the power language has over people.

1. In *I Know Why the Caged Bird Sings* (Angelou), Marguerite's name is changed on a whim by Mrs. Cullinan, who feels the name Marguerite is too long. Have students read the passage aloud:

   > Every person I knew had a hellish horror of being "called out of his name." It was a dangerous practice to call a Negro anything that could be loosely construed as insulting because of the centuries of their having been called niggers, jigs, dinges, blackbirds, crows, boots and spooks.
   >
   > Miss Glory had a fleeting second of feeling sorry for me. Then as she handed me the hot tureen she said, "Don't mind, don't pay no mind. Sticks and stones may break your bones, but words ..." (109)

   In the book, Miss Glory goes on to explain that, twenty years earlier, her name was changed from Hallelujah to Glory by Mrs. Cullinan. Of course, Marguerite is stunned: "Imagine letting some white woman rename you for her convenience" (109). Marguerite then does everything she can to get herself fired.

2. After reading this passage with students, discuss how names are significant. Does the adage about sticks and stones really hold true? How does language hurt, even when the names we are called are not the traditional slurs we consider hurtful? How does our name connect to our identity—and then how important is it to have people call us by our names and not mispronounce or twist them? How does this action of renaming reflect Mrs. Cullinan's character? How does Marguerite's response reflect hers?

   Alternative Suggestion: Any book that deals with name calling or renaming in some way could be used for a similar discussion. *Freak the Mighty* (Philbrick) or *The House on Mango Street* (Cisneros) are two such books.

Shakespeare's Words

New words come into the English language through a variety of avenues: we create new words to meet new needs, borrow them from other languages, or use processes such as shortening to acronyms and alphabetisms (Curzan and Adams 484). Students could even consider how they now use *Google* as a verb for searching on the internet as an example of word change. They could consider other words that have moved from one use to another.

One of the challenges to understanding Shakespeare for many students is the language—and not all of it is syntax. Some of it is vocabulary. Shakespeare is credited with creating more than 1,000 words (McQuain and Malless viii), many that we still use today. He created most of his new words through a "handful of word-making practices" (x): by using them as different parts of speech, by combining words never combined before, and by using prefixes and suffixes in unique ways. Part of understanding Shakespeare means understanding the language of his day, how it has changed since, and how the English language is changed because of him.

1. Introduce the topic of language in Shakespeare by having a discussion of a word common to many of his plays. In *Romeo and Juliet* (Shakespeare), Gregory uses the word *marry* in a way that students often find confusing. Read a passage where the word is found (e.g., 1.1.39) and ask students what it sounds like the term might mean without looking in the text notes. Most of the time, my students say it sounds like a swear word or some slang term. Notes in my text show that the students are close to the mark: it means "indeed (originally an oath to the Virgin Mary)" (15). Students can see that the spelling has already changed through time (*Mary* to *marry*) and we no longer use the word at all; we have a different one (*indeed*) instead. Ask students to think of other words that are an abbreviated version or name of something else and we use like slang; *John Doe* comes to mind as the name for an anonymous person.

2. Share with students the cartoon of Calvin and his mother using Shakespearean language shown in Figure 3.1. Have students translate the dialogue into modern language and discuss the differences they see. Then, have them take a different comic strip (one with character interaction) and rewrite it using Shakespearean language. Sharing these as a class can help students overcome some of the fear they feel and become more comfortable with Elizabethan language.

FIGURE 3.1. Calvin and Hobbes cartoon: Shakespearean language. (CALVIN AND HOBBES © 1992 Watterson. Reprinted with permission of ANDREWS MCMEEL SYNDICATION. All rights reserved.)

3. As they continue to read *Romeo and Juliet*, encourage students to consider unfamiliar words from the perspective of language change. Are these words still in use today? If so, how are they changed? If not, what do we have to replace them? An example might be the word *marrow*, which most students think means *tomorrow*. According to the online *Oxford English Dictionary*, it more likely meant *morning*, but it can also mean *tomorrow*. Because Shakespeare had the option of *morn* (more common in his day than *morning*) or *morrow* (more common in his day than *tomorrow*), why choose what he chose?

    The following are words and phrases coined by Shakespeare to which teachers can draw students' attention in *Romeo and Juliet*. These terms show how language grows. Other words that we no longer use, found in the margins of most versions of the play, can be shown as examples of how language fades.

    - In act 2, scene 4, lines 71–73, Mercutio uses the phrase "wild-goose chase" to describe their witty exchange—coined to resemble the way one goose leads another in formation and later connoting the idea of futility, according to McQuain and Malless.

    - In act 1, scene 3, line 76, the Nurse uses the phrase "man of wax" in describing Paris to Juliet. In other words, he was a model figure, in those days made of wax (such as in a wax museum of famous people). My students are always intrigued by the term. Discuss who might qualify as a "man of wax" today—and what term(s) we use for such people today (McQuain and Malless).

    - I first heard the term *burning daylight* in a John Wayne movie. I thought it was a term used by cowboys. Imagine my surprise to find the term used in *Romeo and Juliet* (1.4.43) and cited by the online *Oxford English Dictionary* as being coined by Shakespeare. The phrase means "to waste time," and Romeo's friends use it when they are on their way to the party where Romeo and Juliet will meet. Students can discuss why the term is used (relating to *burning lamps*) and why we might not use it so much today. Why was it more appropriate, say, for cowboys?

Alternative Suggestion: Reading any of Shakespeare's plays allows for plenty of talk about language change—both growth and decline. *The Scarlet Letter* (Hawthorne) and *The Crucible* (Miller) are two other works often taught in English classes that allow us to address language change, because each text uses words that are no longer commonly spoken today. Giving students the opportunity to research the origins of words is also beneficial in helping them learn about language change—and see it as a natural process.

Rhetorical Grammar

Structure and Meaning

In *Night* (Wiesel), there is one passage in particular that can be used to exemplify the use of text passages to teach *rhetorical grammar*—this is, to show how texts can help students understand that rhetorical choices are important to meaning. This may be a more powerful example than some other texts provide, but all good pieces of literature have passages that can be studied for the rhetorical effects of the grammatical choices found in them. The processes for any passage would be similar; only the choices and effects would differ.

1. Begin by reading the passage with students:

    Never shall I forget that night, the first night in camp, that turned my life into the one thing seven times sealed.
    Never shall I forget that smoke.
    Never shall I forget the small faces of the children whose bodies I saw transformed into smoke under a silent sky.
    Never shall I forget those flames that consumed my faith forever.
    Never shall I forget the nocturnal silence that deprived me for all eternity of the desire to live.
    Never shall I forget those moments that murdered my God and my soul and turned my dreams into ashes.
    Never shall I forget those things, even were I condemned to live as long as God Himself.
    Never.

2. After reading the passage, ask students how it makes them feel. This exploration of emotional response is important so that they can connect what they feel to the choices the writer makes. The passage comes right after Wiesel and his father think they are going to die, but, at the last moment, are instead herded into the barracks. His father reminds him of the woman on the train who screamed about the fires; they had assumed she was insane. They knew now that she was not. This passage is a powerful way of saying that what they experienced is beyond words, beyond description. It can only be conveyed through this moving commentary—and students feel the

weight of the passage, even if they sometimes lack the words to describe their emotions.

3. Next ask students what they notice grammatically about the text. They generally notice what you expect they will: the repeated use of "Never shall I forget" at the start of every statement—and then "Never" by itself at the end. Ask them why Wiesel didn't say "I shall never forget" instead. Usually, students decide that putting the word *Never* first is more powerful than *I* would be. Wiesel wants the eternity of his memory to be emphasized, and his deliberate syntactical choices create that effect.

Students may ask about the use of *shall* instead of *will* in this passage. This is an interesting question. The "rule" is that *shall* is used in the first person—*I shall*—and *will* is used in second and third person—*you will, he will*—to portray simple future. However, both my dictionary and my usage books suggest that this "rule" is rarely followed in actual speech, especially in the United States and especially among younger speakers. As such, sometimes students think its use here is formal or old-fashioned. They wonder if that was intentional. Good question. In some cases, because the rule is so seldom followed in regular use, *shall* can also connote the inevitable or something that must occur. Because *Night* is a translation, it's not clear whether the translator adhered to usage rules, if the original had the sense of *shall* more than *will*, or if the speaker is being formal. Discuss the options with students—but it's hard to say for sure whether this is a rhetorical choice. We can discuss only the effects, not whether those effects were deliberately caused, which brings up another interesting point!

Sometimes students wonder about the formatting of the passage. Because the rest of the book is not formatted this way, but more like a novel, we can assume the formatting (indenting each statement as a paragraph) is deliberate. Discuss with students the effect of single-sentence paragraphs, even single-word paragraphs. Paragraphs are a concept students think they know by the time they read *Night*: each contains five to seven sentences, has a topic sentence, and is focused on a single idea.

But, as Schuster notes, "the reality [is] that there is no such thing as *the* paragraph" (*Breaking* 144). Through examples, he shows that paragraphing changes depending on what genre is being written. I tell my students that paragraphs are the writer's way to tell the reader to consider certain ideas together and then other ideas together and so on. It's a way to control how the ideas are connected in the mind of the reader. So, if Wiesel wants each sentence to be separate rather than connected, he is telling us something with that choice. Have students consider what that might be. They usually conclude that he wants each image to be considered separately, not as part of the whole. In that way, the experience becomes fragmented but also more intense. Readers aren't allowed to crowd the whole experience into a neat package. It must be considered in this broken way.

4. Finally, ask students to notice, if they haven't already, the content of the statements. They sometimes have to be guided to discover that the images, after the first general statement, move from concrete to abstract: smoke, faces, flames, silence, moments, things. This, too, is a rhetorical choice, and students can consider why Wiesel would put the statements in this particular order. If necessary, read them in the reverse order, so students can feel the difference. Most of the time, students decide that starting with the abstract is less powerful, that they need the concrete images first so that they have something to hold onto before they get to the *silence* and the *moments* and the *things*. Thinking about the levels of abstraction, and how they create rhetorical effects, is helpful to them as readers.

5. In informal writing, have students reflect on how the rhetorical choices Wiesel made in this passage enhance the meaning of the passage and, ultimately, the book (at least to this point). Their reflections can aid them in understanding the text more fully.

Alternative Suggestion: Although the choices of rhetorical devices and effects change, many texts lend themselves to this type of questioning process as a way to understand texts better. Any passage that has emotional impact usually has devices and structure that contribute to that impact. Letting students discover those devices and structure in relation to the emotions they find in them builds their sense of rhetorical grammar. I have found *The House on Mango Street* (Cisneros) useful toward this end. The chapter titled "Those Who Don't" (28) is a good follow-up to the *Night* passage because it uses repetition and both abstract and concrete images to express emotion. I find the chapter titled "My Name" (10–11) is also a good one to use to teach how rhetorical grammar influences interpretation. Looking at the rhetorical choices in that chapter (the contrasting positive and negative nouns and adjectives) helps students uncover Cisneros's feelings about her name and the way they are complicated by those feelings about her heritage and new environment. I have also used this process with *An American Childhood* (Dillard), particularly the moth passage (160–62). By asking students to stop and notice the repetition of *wings*, they see how Dillard uses that repetition to emphasize the damage done to the moth. The contrasting verbs *crawled* and *walked*, used against the repetition of *wings* (suggesting flight), give the passage much of its intensity. Usually, the key points of any well-written text benefit from this type of inquiry, and the inquiry helps students gain insight into the meaning of texts.

Sentence Type and Tone

Helping students understand how the choice of sentence types can create an effect in writing can help them avoid the common lapse into imperatives in analysis essays or other school genres. Such lapses suggest that students have learned the idea that sentence types affect tone. A passage in *The Trumpet of the Swan* (White 47–48) allows teachers and students to explore this effect of sentence types and punctuation on tone.

1. To begin, students should have some idea of the four functions of sentences: declarative, interrogative, imperative, and exclamatory. Introduce the idea by asking students what we try to do with sentences. Most students will say "tell someone something" or "ask questions." They might not see difference between explaining (*declarative*), giving directions (*imperative*), and expressing strong emotion (*exclamatory*), as these all seem to combine under a common idea of telling someone something. In fact, Tufte calls imperative, exclamatory, and even interrogative sentences "common reshapings of the basic declarative sentence" (205). Some grammar books differentiate among the sentence types by talking about the punctuation that ends each type—but this seems too simplified and is going to be contradicted by the examples from *The Trumpet of the Swan*. It seems more logical to explain that the differences between sentence types have to do with the intent of the speaker, not the punctuation at the end of the sentence.

2. After students have a sense of the four sentence functions, ask them to consider how the sentences are spoken—that is, what they sound like when people use them. If you have a few examples, such as the following, it might help if students read them aloud, emphasizing the emotion or sense of the sentence:

    - What did you say?
    - How are you getting to the game?
    - I didn't mean it!
    - Hooray!
    - I have to take a test in English class today.
    - I am not going to be able to go to the dance after school.

- Get back in the car.
- Put your books under your desk.

From reading these aloud (along with others the teacher or students might add), students begin to see the tonal qualities associated with different kinds of sentences. Students might benefit from a discussion of how the different sentences make them feel. How do they feel when all they hear is imperatives? "Get in your seat." "Take out your book." "Don't talk." "Read to page 47." On the other hand, does tone change when commands are phrased as declarative sentences? "It is time to get in your seat." "You should have your book out." "It's important that we are all quiet so everyone can study." "The assignment is to read page 47." Ask students: Is it the request or the way the request is made (the sentence construction) that makes the difference in tone?

3. Next, have students read the passage from the novel. It may be helpful to have this one passage prepared to display on a screen so that students can work on it together. On these pages, the cob is trying to help the cygnets fly:

> "I think," said the cob, "the best plan is for me to demonstrate flying to you. I will make a short exhibition flight while you watch. Observe everything I do! Watch me pump my neck up and down before the takeoff! Watch me test the wind by turning my head this way and that! The takeoff must be into the wind—it's much easier that way. Listen to the noise I make trumpeting! Watch how I raise my great wings! See how I beat them furiously as I rush through the water with my feet going like mad! This frenzy will last for a couple of hundred feet, at which point I will suddenly be airborne, my wings still chopping the air with terrific force but my feet no longer touching the water! Then watch what I do! Watch how I stretch my long white elegant neck out ahead of me until it has reached its full length! Watch how I retract my feet and allow them to stream out behind, full length, until they extend beyond my tail! Hear my cries as I gain the upper air and start trumpeting! See how strong and steady my wingbeat has become! Then watch me bank and turn, set my wings, and glide down! And just as I reach the pond again, watch how I shoot my feet out in front of me and use them for the splashdown, as though they were a pair of water skis! Having watched all this, then you can join me, and your mother, too, and we will all make a practice flight together, until you get the hang of it. Then tomorrow we will do it again, and instead of returning to the pond, we will head south to Montana. Are you ready for my exhibition flight?" (White 47–48)

4. After reading the passage, ask students to discuss the tone of the paragraph. What does it feel like? Many should note that the passage feels demanding; they will soon see that this is created by the heavy dependence on imperatives. Students might also note the use of exclamation points, which add a sense of urgency to the passage. Go through the passage with the students and identify the kinds of sentences in it. There are three. The first two are declarative; then begins a series of three imperatives before another declarative is used. This pattern of three imperatives followed by a declarative is repeated. Many imperatives follow the repeated pattern before the final sentences, which are declarative and interrogative. When students have identified the sentences by purpose, they can begin to notice that, even when imperatives don't begin with the verb, they still carry a commanding tone.

5. To further understand the effect, have students change most of the declaratives to imperatives, making the paragraph even more demanding. Then have students change as many of the imperatives as they can to declaratives and discuss the different tone. (In order not to make this task too burdensome, have students work in pairs on one sentence each. They get practice, and the class gets the new passage rewritten quickly so that discussion can focus on the effect more than the rewriting.)

   At this point, students should also look at the punctuation's effect on tone. Most of the time we encourage students to use exclamation points sparingly. Have them consider why White chose not to follow that advice in this passage. They should also be directed to note that one declarative sentence also ends with an exclamation point (the long sentence that ends the second pattern of three imperatives). Ask students what tone is created in this passage by the use of exclamation points.

6. Finally, contrast the following passage with one from the preceding page where the cob is explaining flying. This passage where he is explaining flying has a very different tone (and predominant sentence type) than the passage where he is giving verbal directions for flying. Have students read both passages and explain the differences.

   "True," replied the cob. "But flying is largely a matter of having the right attitude—plus, of course, good wing feathers. Flying consists of three parts. First, the takeoff, during which there is a lot of fuss and commotion, a lot of splashing and rapid beating of wings. Second, the ascent, or gaining of altitude—this requires hard work and fast wing action. Third, the leveling-off, the steady

Extending Your Knowledge

In his article, Schuster identifies several reasons for using fragments. Some of those reasons include "to create a dramatic pause for emphasis," "to create intense emphasis and succinctness," "to emphasize the individual items in a list or series," and "to achieve a more natural conversational tone" ("A Fresh Look" 80–81). I find Schuster's argument compelling—and its application to student writing effective. Certainly, as Schuster explains, students should have a justification for their use of fragments, but, if we're teaching them to consider published writing as mentor texts and then telling them to avoid some of the options available from that mentoring, our instruction seems weakened. Right?

elevated flight, high in air, wings beating slower now, beating strongly and regularly, carrying us swiftly and surely from zone to zone as we cry ko-hoh, ho-ho, with all the earth stretched out far below." (46)

The tone of this passage is so different that students should be able to see that using declaratives—*implied, at least*—creates a different feeling for a reader than using imperatives does. Have them discuss the reasons for that difference. Finally, have students reflect on what thinking about these sentence types means for them as readers and writers. Why might White have made the sentence choices he did? What effects did he want those sentences to have on his readers? What kind of writing has more or fewer of the different types? When can students use their understanding of sentence types to help them as readers?

Because other structures add to the tone of this last passage, be prepared to address concepts such as *fragments, appositives, absolutes, participles,* and *adjectival phrases* that also contribute to this effective passage. Especially with regard to fragments (or what some call *minor sentences*), consider Schuster's review of the best essays in America, which showed that those writers use such constructions frequently. He argues for teaching students the effective uses of fragments used strategically in most of what they read ("A Fresh Look").

Alternative Suggestion: This approach can be used with any text that has passages that vary sentence types to create different tones. Informational texts of different types (e.g., directions and explanation) can be contrasted to emphasize the tonal qualities of sentence types. Students could also investigate the effects of the various sentence types in the description of Catherine's delirium in *Wuthering Heights* (Brontë). In that scene (Chapter 12), the combination of different types of sentences—declarative, interrogative, imperative, and exclamatory—helps to create the sense of madness that lets readers understand her condition.

Repetition and Tone

A Tale of Two Cities (Dickens) provides an effective way to teach about rhetorical devices and the effects they can have on the tone of a piece of writing. Although Myers argues that "reading symbolic meaning out of syntactic structures remains a sketchy and subjective business at best" (18), rhetoricians from ancient times until today have written about the effects of such choices.

1. Read aloud the first two paragraphs of *A Tale of Two Cities* and ask students what they notice about them. They should note the rhythm or repetition. On a screen, have them consider the passage line by line—a format that should help them identify the parallelism and antithesis:

    It was the best of times,
    It was the worst of times,
    It was the age of wisdom,
    It was the age of foolishness,
    It was the epoch of belief,
    It was the epoch of incredulity,
    It was the season of Light,
    It was the season of Darkness,
    It was the spring of hope,
    It was the winter of despair,
    We had everything before us,
    We had nothing before us,
    We were all going direct to Heaven,
    We were all going direct the other way. (13)

Extending Your Knowledge

In *More Grammar to Get Things Done*, Crovitz and Devereaux provide a chart in the appendix (they call it a "grammar shortcut sheet"; 181–84) that lists several grammatical structures with examples and possible effects. For teachers who feel a little nervous about these conversations with students, connecting rhetorical choices with possible effects, this chart would be a good starting place. Of course, some of the effects on readers might depend on the content and context, but this seems like a good foundation for teachers to use.

2. Ask students what effect the structure has on tone. My students sometimes comment that they thought they weren't supposed to repeat things,
especially the beginning of sentences, a belief Bresler finds that can lead
to ridiculous uses of language, to a condition that he calls "the synonym
game" (68). Help students understand that repetition can be carried to
extremes and can be ineffective at times, but that it can also be used effectively. In this passage, the repetition eventually ends with Dickens's statement that "things in general were settled forever" (13). Students should
consider both what the passage is saying as well as the way it is being said:
Are things really settled forever? Is the world of the novel as ordered as
these statements suggest? How does the structure of the passage add to
its meaning? You might remind them that scholars suggest that parallelism reflects logic and orderly thinking (Corbett and Connors) and ask how
knowing that adds to what they think the structure contributes to tone.

3. After studying the effects of the sentences written as they exist, have
students try to write the sentences in different ways and then contrast
their versions with the original to understand further how the grammar
contributes to meaning. They might write, "It was both the best and worst
of times" or "At the same time it was both good and bad, people were
both wise and foolish." After completing the novel, have students return
to these first paragraphs and reconsider structure and tone: now that they
know the story, how are the emphasis and repetition in the beginning even
more important to the meaning of the book?

Alternative Suggestion: Any text that has passages with strong parallelism
or repetition could be used similarly. Often, State of the Union speeches or inaugural addresses use parallelism to create a tone of trust and stability (John F.
Kennedy used these devices regularly). Rylant's *Scarecrow* is also a good text for
highlighting effective repetition, showing both *anaphora* (repetition of beginning

Extending Your Knowledge

In addressing the ridiculous lengths to which writers might go to avoid repetition, Ken
Bresler quotes from an article published in *The Boston Globe* about a "pumpkin-growing
contest." The writer, trying to avoid repeating the word *pumpkin*, referred to "the huge,
orange produce item" (68). Although I know students can go overboard either with
repeating or avoiding repetition, drawing attention to effective uses of repetition in their
reading should go a long way in helping them see this as a valuable tool for reading and
writing. Writers use repetition to make connections, to enhance meaning; our students
can use it in those ways, too.

words or phrases) and *epistrophe* (repetition of concluding words and phrases). Students can consider the way that repetition works to depict a particular tone in any piece and then decide whether it's appropriate for the passage.

English Language Learners and Testing

Language is the tool of my trade.
And I use them all—all the Englishes I grew up with.

—*Amy Tan*

For about five months during my junior year of college, I attended school in Paris, France. Prior to that semester, I had had several years of high school French and two years of college French. When I first arrived in Paris, thinking I knew something of the language, I was rudely awakened: I could barely make myself understood—and I could rarely understand anyone else. Oh, I could recognize a word here and there, and I could point at items on a menu ("Ça") to get what I wanted—if I was in a place where I could point. But no. I wasn't by any stretch of the imagination fluent, even if I thought I was before I went.

By the time I left, though, things were different. I felt confident that I could understand and speak French adequately, if not well. I could ask for directions, find my way, communicate with clerks and waitresses and gendarmes. I had met several French students of my age, and we socialized. I went to French movies and plays. I could visit with the concierge in my building and felt comfortable wherever I went, knowing that, if I didn't speak the language well, I could at least do what I needed to do.

I recently returned to Paris many years after my schooling there. My French, to put it mildly, was rusty. Is there a stage beyond rusty? Disintegrating? Maybe that is what I was. At first, it took me a long time to formulate the questions I needed to ask or the requests I wanted to make. I could only vaguely understand the responses I received. But I found my understanding and ability with the language coming back rather quickly. After ten days, I was dreaming in French again! Both times, though, my experience as a second-language learner made me realize some things about learning another language that help me understand something more about English language learners (ELLs) in my classroom. I liked people to correct me sometimes, but I liked them to do it helpfully, not rudely. I didn't like them to treat me as though I was unintelligent, just because I couldn't remember the gender of a particular noun or the appropriate conjugation of a verb. I found that, when I asked for something incorrectly in a shop and the clerk repeated the request correctly but as a question, I learned without feeling judged. And I appreciated when people waited while I formed sentences and questions, showing appreciation that I was trying to speak their language.

The number of ELLs in US schools is increasing. Mitchell reports that the numbers are now at 4.9 million, up 28 percent since 2000, and up in forty-three states ("The Nation's English-Learner Population"). Even without the statistical evidence, teachers in many classrooms already know the challenge of teaching English classes with increasing percentages of ELLs. A teacher I sat next to a few years ago from Indianapolis told me that her classes had shifted in the last decade from having one or two English learners in her class to being the reverse: only one or two who have English as their first language. The pressure on schools and teachers who have not historically faced the concerns of teaching English to ELLs is great. The related issues can no longer be considered a regional or local concern.

At the same time, public concerns for accountability have raised pressures to measure student achievement in language, both written and spoken. As a result, most states have tests in place that are supposed to measure this achievement. Consequently, not only are ELLs on the spot, but so are native English speakers who may use dialects or vernacular language that doesn't conform to the kind of language being measured in the tests. We also have to concern ourselves with teaching a dialect of English to native speakers: formal or academic English. In this way, the concerns about preparing students for tests and helping ELLs gain proficiency with the language overlap. Both require classrooms where the best practices for thinking about, learning, and using language are employed.

Extending Your Knowledge

Teachers who find their classes increasingly populated with students for whom English is not their first language sometimes panic, wondering what practices they should use to help these students learn. Andrews assures us, "Certified ELL teacher are not wizards of the arcane: They modify successful, proven practices in order to meet the needs of their students" (325). We can do that.

English Language Learners

Because of the growing numbers of ELLs in classes across the United States, more and more information is available to teachers about how we can help our classrooms become places that value those students' home languages at the same time as we help them acquire English-language skills that will bring them success. Haussamen suggests that teachers first need to have a sense of the differences among languages. In *Grammar Alive!*, he and other members of NCTE's Assembly for the Teaching of English Grammar provide an accessible overview of some of the most common languages we meet with students in our classrooms. In summary, Haussamen provides the following list of ways that those languages may diverge from English:

1. The nouns might take gender.

2. Other languages may use articles differently, or no articles at all.

3. Plurals may be formed by adding words or syllables to the sentence, or by giving context clues in the sentence. . . .

4. The word order may not follow the familiar subject-verb-object pattern.

5. The pronoun may not have to agree in gender or number with its antecedent.

6. Other languages may have fewer prepositions, making it confusing for the novice to know which preposition to use in English. Also, the preposition may not precede its object.

7. There are differences in inflection and pacing.

8. There are differences in written conventions, such as punctuation and capitalization.

9. Nonverbal communications, such as gesture, eye contact, silences, and what people do to indicate that they understand, differ from culture to culture. (55)

Extending Your Knowledge

Because, as a teacher, I often feel that I can't learn enough fast enough to be the best teacher to my ELLs, I am reassured by the following sentence from *Grammar Alive!*: "The first and best way to differentiate instruction for your ESL students is to be a gracious host to them in the classroom" (Haussamen 51). That I can do!

By knowing these basic differences, I am better able to understand why ELLs in my classroom use the constructions they do in their writing. As a result, I am better able to help them learn. In addition to learning about the differences among languages, Lee urges teachers to know something about the students and their first languages: "Only after teachers recognize what communicative resources students bring with them, can they begin to successfully help them acquire the language rules of the classroom" (919). Research suggests that students' understanding of their first language may have some impact on their acquisition of the second language (Harmon and Wilson; Heck). And teachers who know something about the students, about their background and their interests, can select instruction and activities that will most benefit those students' acquisition of language in the classroom.

Besides teachers who care about them and learn something about them, what else do ELLs need to gain language skills in our classrooms? One big thing is time. We need to remember that language acquisition is a lengthy process and that there might be backsliding and uneven development before any significant progress is recognized. The updated "NCTE Position Paper on the Role of English Teachers in Educating English Language Learners (ELLs)" acknowledges that gaining fluency in a second language is a gradual process, with many of the recommendations suggesting practices that occur over time as students build on their understanding of their native language and gain skills and content knowledge in the second language.

Many of the recommendations for teaching ELLs from the NCTE position paper are what teachers should recognize as good instructional practices for all our students. To begin, we need to engage all students, but especially ELLs, in lots of language use—in both oral and written forms. Students need to engage in large- and small-group discussions. Christy suggests pairing students, a native English speaker with an English-learning student, and having them make short, informal presentations to the class about idioms or colloquialisms that may be confusing to the ELLs but necessary to their communication skills. I know that, when I was in Paris, I would hear phrases that didn't seem to make sense (e.g., they say it's "raining ropes" or "raining frogs" instead of "raining cats and dogs," as Americans do, to describe heavy rain). When I heard these phrases or terms, I would write them down and take them to a French friend who spoke some English and who lived upstairs from us. He would explain the meaning so that I was able to learn more about the everyday uses of French than I learned in my classes.

Since that experience, we have become friends with a young couple from Bolivia, in the United States to study English. In addition to our conversations, we often use apps like FaceTime, or more frequently Marco Polo, so that, when we find ourselves using an idiom that they may not know, we quickly record a short video about it that we think they might find useful. Likewise, when they hear an idiom or usage they find confusing, they immediately send us a Marco Polo, asking about meaning. This kind of access is key to developing fluency, and teachers might be able to encourage that in their classes. By spending a few minutes of class time explaining idioms and expressions, teachers not only help develop ELLs' understanding of English, but they also help native speakers learn something about their own language. I know that is true of our sharing with our Bolivian friends—I have become much more aware of the frequency of idioms in our everyday language.

Besides reading everyday texts such as websites and functional texts (bulletins, direction, etc.), we can use literature to help ELLs learn more about English. Kooy and Chiu assert that "literature—a place where language and culture meet—offers a significant source" for what they call a "broader vision" for helping ELLs gain fluency with language (79). "Literature," they continue, "merits its own place in ESL teaching and learning—not only for its intrinsic worth, but as an integral part of a language learning program" (79). We should choose literature that will help students learn about language as well as about the context in which that language occurs. The NCTE position paper encourages teachers to "recogniz[e] that literacy growth increases with both abundant exposure to reading and a variety of texts as well as explicit literacy instruction" (National Council of Teachers of English sec. 4, par. 2).

Literature—both traditional as well as picture books—should be read aloud to students, at least some of the time. That way, students can hear the way language in literature sounds. Reading aloud can help students understand more than they do when reading silently because teachers' inflections and the connections to illustrations (in picture books) can help students understand more than their language level might normally allow. This is true for native speakers, as well. When I read parts of *The Right Stuff* aloud to my juniors, many of my native English speakers expressed how much better they understood the text because they could hear it as they were reading. Keeping the learning about literature social, through discussions, also helps develop students' facility with language. Such discussions, in small and large groups, help students understand what Fagan urges as important to all students, not just ELLs: "that the words on the page should be *thought* about and not just decoded" (38). Kooy and Chiu note that "texts alone do not change ESL classes or mystically improve language. *How the texts are read and shared* brings language to life and life to the literature"

(82, emphasis added). Among other points, the NCTE position paper (sec. 4, par. 3) makes the following recommendations for teaching literature, many of which are effective practices teachers use regularly:

- Select texts that are accessible to students at a range of reading proficiencies.
- Explicitly teach reading comprehension strategies.
- Relate the topic to students' cultural experiences.
- Consider having students read a more accessible text such as a graphic novel or watch a video before reading the assigned text.
- Conduct prereading activities that activate prior knowledge.
- Consider teaching texts as part of a genre study.

Frequent writing in a variety of genres also helps students develop their language skills. By writing informally, students are able to express themselves without worrying about every aspect of written language—thus developing fluency and the ability to convey thoughts through writing. Using mentor texts helps students extend the range of options they see available to them as writers. The choices of the types of texts we ask students to write can be an important consideration for ELLs.

One text that I have used successfully is *My House Has Stars* (McDonald). With this text that explores homes around the world, students do some research and write about a place that is important to them. Using words and images specific to that place, students write and share their short pieces, which I compile into a class book that we can all enjoy. My own experience and that of teachers who have also had their students write with this text as a mentor is that it is especially motivating for our ELLs. They get to share their past, their culture, and some words from their first language, and these aspects make the writing appealing to students. I wrote about it in *Voices from the Middle* (Dean, "Framing"), and a lesson based on the article is available on the ReadWriteThink website (Gardner). The lesson builds on the article and provides further suggestions for using mentor texts to help ELLs learn to use inquiry in their writing through a scaffolded plan.

Clearly, writing is essential to students' development with English, but correcting many errors in that writing may not achieve what teachers hope it will. Teachers' comments on more formal writing should be explicit and clear to help students understand where their use of written language doesn't communicate as well as it could. In terms of correcting, though, repeated studies show that grammar correction does not necessarily result in improved use of the corrected concepts in further writing and probably is an ineffective use of teachers' time (Gray; Loewen). Even with native English speakers, such corrections often don't achieve what we hope they will when we write comments to students about their writing, but, with ELLs, our comments may suffer additional communication barriers. It might be more effective to give students lots of opportunities to write for different purposes and audiences—purposes and audiences determine many features of writing, including different levels of correctness with language. Students can use informal writing to take risks. With formal writing, teachers might focus on a specific aspect to work on improving, instead of feeling that every misuse of language should be addressed.

The NCTE position paper (sec. 4, par. 2) also makes the following recommendations for teachers teaching writing to ELLs:

- Provide a nurturing writing environment.
- Use mentor texts.
- Encourage collaboration in writing.
- Give frequent opportunities to write in a variety of genres and for a variety of purposes.
- Teach strategies for helping writers use the writing process.
- Use both teacher and peer feedback.
- Make comments clear and explicit.

Again, most of these suggestions are effective for all the students in our classes.

The position paper also makes a specific recommendation for ELLs about *translanguaging*—the use of a person's full linguistic repertoire. This approach encourages students who have another language to use that language to their advantage in their learning in English classes. This could mean taking notes in a combination of languages, but it could also mean blending language in some of the reading and writing students do in their classes. Students might use mobile devices to access online dictionaries or translators, but they might also use other digital tools to support their language development, such as games or videos.

Besides being given the opportunity to use writing to develop their language skills, ELLs also need to know the language of academics—but this is also something that all students need. In fact, academic English (even Standard English) is a dialect that many of our students, including native English speakers, may need to learn. Because this dialect of English is not what we hear regularly (it's probably only written for the most part), many researchers (e.g., Heck; Horning) suggest that what may be the best way for all students—ELLs, speakers of a vernacular form of English, or students who haven't had much exposure to academic texts—to learn academic language is to approach it as a second language, or, as Hagemann calls it, a "second dialect" ("Balancing" 73). As she notes, "learning 'school talk' is a monumental task" (73). The NCTE position paper suggests that teachers engage students in considering when writers would need to use this variety of English and then be sure to teach key discourse structures that are typical of academic language. It also recommends "maintaining the rigor and complexity of academic tasks" while helping students learn how to show their ability to write in academic ways about academic topics, not waiting for students to "have mastered certain grammatical structures" (National Council of Teachers of English sec. 9, par. 4).

As I have noted and much of the research suggests, good instruction for ELLs is also good instruction for native English speakers (Andrews; Burke; Harmon and Wilson). If we are aware of the differences in the languages students come to class with—whether that is another language or a dialect of English— and if teachers come to know their students, their choices of effective practice will benefit all students as they develop facility with and awareness of multiple levels of language use.

Preparing for Tests

Because tests differ on what they expect students to know, it's important for teachers to know what their own state's test will assess students on. Some states are more traditional and others less so in their approaches to what they see as achievement in language. States may test a variety of aspects of language, such as usage, punctuation, spelling, syntax, levels of formality, even structures of paragraphs and essays. Some states ask students to identify parts of speech (nouns, adjectives, or prepositions) or parts of sentences (subjects and predicates) on tests, while others ask students to select the "correct" sentence from a list of options.

If a test asks for parts of speech, students will need to know those, and—despite how we might feel about teaching traditional definitions and concepts—we do students a disservice if we fail to help them learn what they need to succeed on the tests. We can and should work to make changes in those tests, to help those who make the tests or who mandate them understand best practice. In the meantime, though, we should also use best practice when we prepare students for tests. For me, that means not spending all of class time on test preparation but, instead, helping my students put what they need to know to succeed on the test in perspective with the other aspects of language they should be learning that will extend past the test and into their lives beyond school. For example, if I know they will need to identify adjectives for the test, we might stop and have them notice those and what they do in our reading, as in the dialogue that follows. I can address concepts students will need for large-scale tests—but not as test prep. Instead, I can weave these concepts into my teaching of reading and writing.

TEACHER (*after reading the first four paragraphs of the chapter "Green Stucco House" in* One Crazy Summer *by Williams-Garcia*): Let's pause here for a minute. Big Ma had told Delphine some things about Cecile—about where she lived. Delphine, as she says any six-year-old would, interprets Big Ma's information with a few added details. What are the differences between what Big Ma said and what Delphine envisioned?

MARIA: When she said "on the street," Delphine thought that was real. Like on the tar.

TEACHER: Sure. Let's look at the details there: what kind of tar?

BILLY: Black and gray.

TEACHER: Yes—anyone remember from elementary school what those kinds of words are called? Yes, I know it was a long time ago. Words that tell us details about nouns?

SARAH: Adjectives?

TEACHER: Sure. Adjectives tell us details about the nouns that are close to them. Can you see any other adjectives in that paragraph?

JACK: Broken?

DAX: Skid?

TEACHER: Good.

JILL: Blackened?

TEACHER: Yes. What difference do those adjectives make? I mean, if we just said *tar*, *glass*, *marks*, and *gum*, would it be the same?

JILL: Well, "blackened gum" sounds a lot grosser than just *gum*.

JACK: Yeah. And "broken glass" is worse than just *glass*.

TEACHER: Okay—so what can we say adjectives do for us as readers?

MARIA: It makes a better picture.

SEAN: Yeah. It's kinda like we see the mood, too. Like not just a street, but a street with potholes sounds worse.

TEACHER: So we can see not just pictures, but also a tone from adjectives? (*Murmurs.*) Okay—let's look in the next paragraph and see where the adjectives are and if they are still doing the same thing.

DAX: Pigeon poop! (*Laughs.*)

TEACHER: Okay, yes. A specific kind. What does it tell us, why does that detail matter?

JILL: Park. It's in a park because that's where pigeons live.

TEACHER: Sure. What other adjectives?

MARK: The wino—here it says he's "smelly" and "toothless." That makes him seem worse than just a wino.

TEACHER: Sure. And, in case you didn't notice it, "splintery" park bench as opposed to a regular park bench. So, what do you think this author is trying to tell us, or what Delphine is trying to tell us? Big Ma gave the basics—the nouns—but Delphine added the adjectives. What is she telling us?

SARAH: Well, she said, "when you're six," so I think that might mean that little kids imagine the worst, because all the adjectives make things seem worse.

TEACHER: Is that true? (*Murmurs of assent.*) Okay. Let's see why that matters; let's see where Cecile really lives. (*Continue reading.*)

If a state's test asks students to identify parts of speech, it would be important, first, for teachers in that state to understand that words aren't only one part of speech—the part of speech is determined partly by the function of the word in the sentence. *Grammar Alive! A Guide for Teachers* (Haussamen) gives a good, brief explanation of form, function, and frame to help teachers appropriately address traditional grammar for tests—at the same time as it gives students a useful foundation for moving beyond definitions. Simply teaching the definitions of parts of speech doesn't accomplish what we want, as they are mostly "definitions that do not define" (Schuster, *Breaking* 19). Meyer compares words to pieces of a chess game; the part of speech (or the use of the pawn) isn't always the same—it depends on "the way it fits into the system" (40). Helping students learn that concept will prepare them for the test and will also move them beyond simply thinking of words as belonging to one category or another, unconnected to use.

Beyond the fact that the definitions of parts of speech rarely help students identify, much less use, words correctly, Meyer argues that tests that require students to consider definitions as essential to parts of speech do a disservice to students' understanding of English as a whole because they "[reinforce] the idea that the structure of English is already completely known and is no longer subject to increased understanding or insight. What is being tested here is knowledge, not serious study of English grammar, but of tradition" (38). Helping students understand how to answer the questions on the test about parts of speech is important; helping them understand how that knowledge is only the beginning of understanding the dynamic nature of English is the rest of the story, the big part of the iceberg that is under the water. We don't want to leave students unaware of the immense part of the language that is there for them to discover.

Some tests ask students to identify the correct or "best" sentence from a set of options. These sentences may have issues with punctuation or with grammar or usage (such as pronoun or subject–verb agreement). The ability to select the "correct" sentence from the choices is often seen as evidence of the students'

Extending Your Knowledge

Jim Meyer asserts that "we will not have good instruction in the structure of English unless teachers themselves are curious about it, are trained to observe it, and know where to look for answers" (42). Debra Myhill et al. agree—and so do I. An underlying principle for effective teaching of language in this time of testing has got to be teachers' interest in language, in how it works and what it can do. Only by expanding our view of language, instead of limiting it to what's on tests, will we help students to develop the language skills they need for life.

ability to write well. I know—that doesn't make sense. How can choosing a preconstructed sentence be the same as writing one? But that is what we have. To help them prepare for these types of questions, then, students need to think about and play around with sentences—ones they write and ones they read. We may need to have students take an effective sentence and mix it up, make it part of a test question for the rest of the students in the class, so that they can practice moving from the "correct" to the "incorrect." Will students know how to do this? Probably not at first, but they can learn. And it makes more sense to me that they work with good sentences, sentences that do what they are supposed to do, more than seeing "problem" sentences in three out of every four examples. Plus, my students seem to like to make things "worse." When I ask them to show genre knowledge by writing the Worst Picture Book ever, they engage enthusiastically. They might prefer to create their own test questions as a way to practice—and then see into the mystery of tests from the other direction.

As teachers, we need to develop students' sensitivity to sentences. We can do this, at least in part, by reading aloud to students and commenting on sentences that work well so that students become aware of how effective sentences work. Such practices encourage students to begin to notice effective sentences themselves. Even if they don't write them, the practice will help them on tests that ask them to simply pick the most effective sentence—not write one. Developing that sensitivity will help them when sentences like the following are among their choices:

I see the park going to school every day.
Which is the best way to write this sentence?
    A. Every day I see the park going to school.
    B. I see the park on the way to school every day.
    C. Every day I see the park on my way to school.
    D. I see the park every day going to school.
(CSL00142.024 qtd. in California Department of Education 49)

Students would first need to note that the question asks them about *writing* the sentence and not speaking it, because in speech we would all be able to know exactly what the speaker meant. Not many students are going to read the sentence in its original form and really think the park is going to school. The best way to help students with questions like this is to have them hear, read, and think about good sentences—about how they work and the way they convey meaning. In that way, students will develop the sensitivity they need to prepare not only for the tests but also for their own needs as readers and writers.

Do the methods of teaching writing that we use to help students grow as writers work in preparing students for tests of writing that don't ask students to write? Do they even help prepare them for tests that do require writing? Warne speaks to those questions when she addresses Romano's approach to teaching conventions. Romano asserts, "I want students to steadily improve their skills in language and in producing written texts that reflect the norms of standard edited English (and to break those norms when they do so meaningfully)" (74). When Warne argues that Romano "advocates rule breaking for valid communication or artistic purposes—but he was not preparing students for a high stakes test" (24), she makes a good point. How do we help students think about writing as they should—adapting it according to their purposes, audiences, situations, and genres, when what will really matter (at least in the short term) is their ability to correct sentences like the following on a test?

It is easily the best place in the city <u>for: sports,</u> picnics, concerts, walking, and enjoying nature.
How should the underlined part of the sentence be written?
   A. for-sports,
   B. for; sports,
   C. for sports,
   D. for: sports
(CSL00138.024 qtd. in California Department of Education 49)

As Weaver shows in her analysis of American College Testing language questions, many test questions are complex, measuring multiple areas of knowledge about language (*Grammar Plan Book*). Whether or not tests ask for grammatical terms, we need to be aware that a broad exposure to written language with an eye toward noticing what happens in the craft of writing is probably a solid preparation for tests of language. And it benefits students as writers, too.

From experiences described by Smoot and Gold, it's clear that parents and administrators—even students—often want class material to focus directly on the test. Gold describes having parents upset that this teaching, based on research into best practice, didn't seem to be preparing their children to succeed on standardized tests. He acknowledges that "to a parent fearful that his or her child will do poorly on the SAT [Scholastic Aptitude Test], no amount of citing education research is going to allay that fear; we need to make a personal connection" (46). By having parents read their children's writing and see improvement over time, Gold was able to show that his teaching could accomplish both purposes: prepare students for tests and help them improve as writers. Smoot's experience was a little different, perhaps partly because he worked in a different situation. In his school, students also resisted the teaching of grammar integrated into reading and writing, but mostly because they wanted a unit on grammar to have a definite beginning and end.

In addition, Smoot found that having students do well on the standardized tests "meant working at least some of the time within that traditional framework" (39). In other words, the teaching had to match (at least some of the time) the assessment. Even though students' writing and reading abilities improve through effective integrated instruction, testing means we have to think about the test and work at least partly with the goals and principles the tests value and measure. Weaver (*Grammar Plan Book* 64–65) gives the following advice to teachers about how to approach language instruction in terms of testing:

1. Don't abandon best practice in the teaching of writing.

2. Make the most of the overlap between revision and editing skills needed for your state's test.

3. Reserve for test preparation those items that are important for your students, not only for the test but as writers.

4. Use practice test items with students.

5. Teach students to write like published authors and then teach the standardized test's "rules" as part of these.

All of these points are solid. NCTE's position paper on preparing ELLs for tests reinforces the idea that the best preparation for tests is *not* test prep but actually good instruction for general reading and writing skills. The paper (sec. 12, par. 2) adds the following points specifically for students who are also learning English and need to take standardized tests:

• Teach students how to take a prompt apart.

- Teach them how to work effectively in a timed-writing situation.
- Make sure they know how to apply strategies for reading for different purposes to test questions and directions.

I support these suggestions. Students need to know what's expected on the tests—but they also need to know that tests are only one measure of writing ability. If they know that language shifts for different situations—and they know the language needed in the different situations—they should be able to make the adjustment between testing and using language knowledge in other, more authentic situations.

In the lesson ideas that follow, I have tried to consider the needs of ELLs as well as the needs of all students who must adjust language for different situations, including those of testing. I am comforted by the comments of many of the teachers whose writing I've read as I've tried to determine the best approaches for my students who do not have English as their first language or academic English as a dialect. As Burke explains:

> ESL students have unique needs, to be sure, but in many respects, good teaching for one group of students is good for all students, so long as the teacher uses the techniques that move everyone forward regardless of their current ability. ("Learning" 42)

The ideas that follow take into account the general philosophy of language this book promotes as well as what Burke urges. I hope they help every student grow with regard to language understanding and use, especially in high-stakes situations.

Traditional Grammar

Writing a Story Collaboratively

Using the children's book *Fortunately* (Charlip) as a prompt helps students generate sentences and connect them to previous sentences, and it teaches them about adverbs and agreement of pronouns and subjects and verbs. At the same time, students are having fun in a collaborative writing activity—all important aspects of learning language for all learners.

1. Begin by reading the book aloud to the students. It is a story about a boy whose life is punctuated by alternating fortunate and unfortunate events. The events are linked by the two adverbs (*unfortunately* and *fortunately*), and students quickly see the pattern the book establishes.

2. After briefly discussing the book's pattern, have each student write the opening sentence to a story at the top of a piece of paper—a sentence that sounds as if it will bode well for the character mentioned in it and begins "Fortunately." It's important for teachers to know (and to share with students) that this book was published in 1964. Since then, the expectations for comma use after an introductory adverb have shifted. According to current grammar handbooks, each of the sentences should have a comma after the adverb, but the text does not have them. If you show the sentences to students, you might want to make clear the changed expectations so that students will know them for tests and other situations where it will matter. Certainly, you should make students aware of the current expectation so that they can practice it when they write the sentences for their stories.

3. When all the students have written a beginning sentence, have them pass their paper to another student. This student writes the next sentence, which begins "Unfortunately" and complicates the story by showing a negative, unanticipated outcome that links to the first sentence. Continue this process for several sentences, with each student reading the sequence of sentences on the new page they are handed and continuing the pattern of fortunate and unfortunate events. After several passes, have students start writing sentences that seem to circle around to (potentially) resolving the story. The final person should write the last two or three sentences to finish the story. Give the papers back to the original writers and have them share them in small groups.

4. As students read the stories aloud or share them with their groups, they can check for appropriate grammar conventions (punctuation of initial adverbs, subject–verb and pronoun agreement) as well as vote for which story to read to the whole class. Students tend to feel less worried about sharing because the story is a result of group effort. Any "errors" that might exist are fairly anonymous, so you and your students can discuss them without worrying about putting a single person on the spot. By generating the writing that is used for the instruction, students are more invested in their learning about the grammar involved.

Identifying Adjectives and Using Them in Writing

One task some state tests ask students to do is identify adjectives in sentences. Although such a task doesn't have much application outside of a testing situation, students' ability to use adjectives effectively—to communicate clearly and to set a mood—is one that can benefit all student writers. Haussamen also recommends the practice for ELLs.

1. Begin by reading the book *Where the Wild Things Are* (Sendak). At the page where the wild things first appear, stop and have students visualize their own "wild things." Then, have them draw their vision—but the head only—on a piece of 9" × 12" cardstock. Where the mouth of the monster is, have students cut two horizontal slits, at least a 1/2-inch apart and 2 inches long.

2. Next, have students brainstorm words that describe. Talk about the questions adjectives answer—questions about what kind, which one, how many, or what color. You can also help students understand the forms of the words: they can end in -*ed* (such as *iced*) or -*y* (such as *silly*) or -*ing* (such as *bleeding*) or -*ous* (such as *enormous*).

3. After the class brainstorms, have students individually list possible adjectives for their wild things, using words that describe either the appearance or the character. When they have the start of a list, have them work with a partner to generate more word possibilities. After students have a number of possibilities, they should identify the best ten and write them on a strip of paper (just under 2 inches wide and about 10 inches long). The words should be listed just a little more than a 1/2-inch inch apart. When students are done, have them thread the paper through the two slits on the mouth of the monster so that one adjective at a time shows in the mouth. Have students share their wild things and the words they've selected to describe them with each other and with the class.

4. Finally, have students use the adjectives to write a description of their wild things. At this point, I address structures that they can use as alternates to "My monster is *big*," repeated in various forms. We discuss using prepositional phrases ("*enormous*" could become "with an *enormous* mouth"), changing adjectives to adverbs ("*wild* could become "swinging his arms *wild*ly about his head"), or using adjectives out of order ("*green, hairy* monster" could be written as "*green and hairy*, the monster"), in sentences like these that I wrote as an example:

> Some parents or observers might question the appropriateness of this activity for secondary students. Weaver notes that "for some—perhaps many—classes at all grade levels, focusing on sensory detail and the use of precise nouns, verbs, adjectives, and adverbs may be an important prelude to playing around with more sophisticated modifying constructions" (*Grammar Plan Book* 58). It has certainly been my experience that many secondary students need the activities that we think belong only in elementary school in order to gain the learning they still need as older students.

> Shockingly green and hairy, the enormous monster frightened the penguins who had never seen such a furry beast—nor one so colorful. The screeching monster gestured wildly with his four arms while his three long ears bounced like bunnies around his square head.

By isolating the adjectives first and then using them in a variety of ways in their writing, students can begin to see how adjectives work in writing so that, if they need to identify them for a test, they have some idea of the places adjectives live in sentences and the shapes they can take.

Alternative Suggestion: Burke recommends another way to have students use their knowledge of grammar terminology: to annotate directions on tests and assignments. Students underline the verbs in the prompt to make sure they respond appropriately. He explains that "such work up front not only helps students manage the assignment, but reinforces for them that words have a function and that function informs" ("Developing" 58). After annotating prompts a few times, have students write their own directions for an assignment and then trade them with a classmate who annotates the student-generated version to give feedback on verbs.

Editing

Becoming Observant about Punctuation

One of the most obvious ways to help students learn editing skills needed for tests or for formal, academic writing is to have them study punctuation in the texts that they read. To see it, and notice it, and talk about it would be the best preparation they could have. A student teacher I observed had her students stand and use what she called the "Victor Borge method" of punctuating. Following Borge's lively and exaggerated movements when playing the piano, students made large gestures with their arms in the air to emphasize quotation marks, commas, periods, even colons. It was great to watch; students really got into it. Best of all, students really knew their editing and paid more attention to punctuation when they read and wrote.

1. First, help students become observers of punctuation by drawing their attention to it as you read texts together. Doing so will be more meaningful and generally provides better learning than instruction with "rules." For example, looking at sentences from *Long Night Moon* (Rylant) can help students inductively learn the "rule" about commas with coordinating and cumulative adjectives that can be found in *The Brief Penguin Handbook* (Faigley):

    > You can recognize coordinate adjectives by reversing their order; if their meaning remains the same, the adjectives are coordinate and must be linked by *and* or separated by a comma.... Commas are not used between cumulative adjectives, two or more adjectives that work together to modify a noun. (79)

    Following are some sentences from *Long Night Moon*:

    > In June the Strawberry Moon shimmers on succulent buds, on <u>quiet, grateful rabbits</u>.
    > In July the Thunder Moon trembles, shudders, and disappears in a <u>thick, black sky</u>.

    Is it easier to see the "rule" with these sentences than it is with the explanation from the handbook? For me, it is. I think for some students it will be also. You can find additional sentences in the book that also teach the concept—and some that teach other concepts about commas and adjectives.

    Teachers with whom I work do this kind of "observant reading" with all kinds of texts that they read as a class, sometimes extending their observations about a particular use of punctuation across several readings. Their work in this way effectively develops students' abilities to understand punctuation uses.

2. But our work doesn't have to stop at only noticing punctuation in our reading—and some students might need more direction. To prepare students for tests, you might also want to periodically present a question from the test that might provide more direct practice. Although I wouldn't recommend such decontextualized practice regularly (that would be akin to the worksheets that we know didn't work in the past), seeing the type of questions asked in the test and articulating the required responses might benefit some students, especially if students can attach their answers to the observations they've made during reading. And using the test questions

doesn't have to limit my explanation of language in my classroom to simple right or wrong. For instance, I might put up the following test question one day for discussion, just so students will know the kind of multifaceted questions they will be asked:

Dear Mayor Lewis:

How should this be written?

    A. Dear mayor Lewis

    B. Dear Mayor Lewis—

    C. My Dear Mayor Lewis,

    D. Leave as is.

(CSL00139.024 qtd. in California Department of Education 49)

Note that the question requires students to consider punctuation, capitalization, and tone—all in reference to a particular genre, a business letter. Discussing this question can help my students prepare for the test, but it also allows me to talk about how the choice might change if we change the situation—so I get to use the test prep in ways that fit with my overall goals of teaching language for life outside the classroom and not simply of language as right or wrong.

Usage

Teaching Tone through Analogy

One thing many tests measure is the appropriate tone for a piece of writing. Questions may ask students to choose the best way for something to be written, but they are really asking about tone, as in the following:

In paragraph 2, sentence 5 [of Cara Johnson's business letter to Mayor Lewis] begins with the word Kids. How should this be written?

    A. Small children, because it is more formal

    B. Tikes, because it's friendlier

    C. Kids, because that's how people talk

    D. Little kids, because it's more descriptive

(CSW00513.024 qtd. in California Department of Education 49)

Students will need to make a choice based on the idea of whether the word is an appropriate level of formality for the rest of the writing and/or the genre. It's important for them to understand that the answer isn't simple: writers don't always choose the most formal option; nor do they always choose the friendlier, more descriptive or familiar forms. They must fit choice to situation. We can help students understand more about language by contrasting their informal usages with more formal usages.

The ReadWriteThink lesson "Style-Shifting: Examining and Using Formal and Informal Language Styles" provides a good way for teachers to enhance their students' understanding of formality. Its authors, di Gennaro and Schultz, note that "style-shifting is often below our level of consciousness as speaker or writers, but can be problematic for us as listeners or readers" (par. 3). I summarize the key elements here, but teachers can access the resources on the ReadWriteThink lesson plan webpage.

1. Have students explore sample sentences and rate them from 1 to 5 on a scale of *very informal* to *very formal*. Students compare their answers with partners or in small groups and begin to develop a list of features they notice that distinguish different levels of formality.

2. As a class, make a list of different groups of people they interact with regularly and discuss how each group is its own speech community, with its own ways of communicating. Students should find this fairly familiar as they contrast the ways they ask for information in one group as opposed to another. I often note in this discussion that beginning an email to me with "Wassup?" is probably violating the community expectations between teacher and student. I tell them I'm getting used to students starting their emails to me with "Hey!"—but it's taken a while. They find it funny for me to bring these ideas up.

3. Next, have students choose two of the speech communities they interact with—one formal and one informal—and then find examples of interactions they have with these two communities to contrast. They might find emails or texts or other artifacts that will help them in this activity. As they compare and contrast the language levels, they should begin to notice that

they already adjust for levels of formality and can be more intentional about that in their writing.

4. Finally, have students read a short text and write a summary for the teacher. After they have completed the summary, have them write to a "friend" who missed class and tell them about the reading. Then, in small groups, have students discuss the specific examples of adjustments they made for the different levels of formality and draw some conclusions about the types of sentence structures, vocabulary, and sentence length they adjust for levels of formality.

Alternative Suggestion: Teachers can have students write about something simple and straightforward in the more formal language of a science presentation. BAHfest is an example of people who do this (Ullman offers one example). Wisniewski's *Secret Knowledge of Grown-Ups* provides another example of talking about something mundane in a more formal tone that students can consider as mentors for their own practice in adjusting their writing for differing levels of formality—and then reflecting on what they had to do to make the shift in tone (Dean, *Strategic* 154–56).

Pragmatics

Another aspect of language variety we can address with our students comes from the field of linguistics, particularly pragmatics. Hagemann explains *pragmatics* as "a person's understanding of the various linguistic demands of various social contexts" (*Teaching* 116), or, in other words, how we adjust our language for different social situations. Because I'm not a linguist, I can speak only as a novice who finds the topic interesting. But the work on how language shifts for politeness as a reflection of differing relationships, using "various linguistic strategies such as indirectness, hedges, or politeness markers to strategically avoid conflict" (Lee 21–22), is another way to raise students' awareness of language, in general, and in usage, in particular.

1. Begin by explaining to students the idea of politeness as a language concept. Conduct a short discussion about how students ask friends for things as opposed to how they ask a figure of authority—say a principal or police officer. Most students already understand that we make some requests differently, depending on whom we are asking. Expand their understanding by sharing some of the reasons for those differences, as explained by Lee:

Each speech community develops politeness principles from which they derive certain linguistic strategies. The decisions about which strategy is used within a culture depend on how the culture assesses the following three factors: the relative power relationship between speaker and hearer ...; the social distance between speaker and hearer; and the individual ranking of the particular imposition in the social context in which it is used. (23)

2. Next, use an exercise suggested by Wolfram to consider the idea in more depth. Have students rank the following sentences in order of politeness, generally. Have them work individually first, and then in small groups before the whole class discusses the rankings.

> Pass me the butter!
> Can you pass me the butter?
> I would like you to pass the butter.
> You need to pass the butter.
> Would you mind passing the butter?
> Are you using the butter?
> These potatoes could use some butter. ("Linguistic" 105)

There isn't a particular order to this ranking, so it's important to ask students why they made the rankings they did as a way to discuss language and its varieties in different situations. Every time I have conducted this activity, students are amazed that others don't see the statements in the same ranking as they do. The discussion that follows is a great way to open our understanding to how others might interpret our language use.

3. Next, following Wolfram's suggestion, have students generate a list of ways to ask for something else, such as asking someone to open a door or window. By creating their own lists and ranking them, students learn more about language use, how we often create difficulties because of inattention to principles of politeness, and how these principles reflect cultural expectations. Some of these cultural expectations are related to gender, age, or relationship. I sometimes use Calvin and Hobbes comics to help students see how effective communication is a function of relationships. It seems that Calvin sometimes has trouble communicating with his parents—and understanding them. Using examples such as these or ones students bring in can solidify the point about language use.

4. When a class is reading a piece of literature, teachers can reinforce this discussion by asking students to consider a request made by one character to another. How does the way the request is made show the relationship

of the character? In what other way could the character have made the request?

For example, in *One Crazy Summer* (Williams-Garcia), when the girls first meet Cecile, the situation is not comfortable. After flying all day, they arrive at her home in the evening and are hungry. What follows are some of the statements they make:

DELPHINE: "We're hungry.". . .

VONETTA: "What's for supper?"

FERN: "Hungry. Hungry." She rubbed her belly. . . .

CECILE: "What you want from me?"

DELPHINE: "Supper. . . . It's past eight o'clock. We haven't had real food since breakfast." (30–31)

Students should consider how these statements reflect the relationship and what other ways they might have responded to one another if their relationships were different. By connecting pragmatics—social use of language—to the characters and relationships in the literature they read, students learn more about language variation.

Understanding Language through Metaphors

Dong writes about the use of metaphors in English and how they enhance and pervade the language. To most people, metaphors are poetic devices, used mostly in descriptive writing. They are figures of speech we use consciously when we want to sound poetic or musical—or, even, smart. Most of us do not realize how, as Dong asserts, metaphors have "become a part of everyday English" (30). Citing Pollio et al.'s research, she shows how prevalent they are: "It is almost impossible to avoid metaphors in daily life. An average native English speaker uses about five metaphors per hour, and more than 1,000 metaphors per day at the rate of a four-hour speaking day" (30). Nilsen and Nilsen note:

> [The use of metaphors is] universal because human minds all work much the same, and all speakers live in the same real world and so are likely to talk about such things as the head of a company and the teeth of a comb, a rake, or a saw. However, the details may differ because metaphors highlight only a single feature of a comparison, so the speakers of one language might choose to focus on the shape of something, while the speaker of another language might focus on an action. (27)

Because many metaphors in English have parallels in other languages, the study of metaphors not only benefits ELLs' acquisition of English but also gives them opportunities to share aspects of their language with native English speakers. All students benefit as they learn more about language.

1. To begin, students may need a refresher on *metaphors*. In the most basic sense, they are implied comparisons—one thing associated with another. They are distinguished from similes by the fact that similes make a direct comparison through words such as *like* or *as*. Metaphors can be stated somewhat directly, usually using a *be* verb: "That man is a snake." They can also be implied—and these implied metaphors can be trickier for students. Murfin and Ray explain it this way:

    > The thing being represented by the metaphor is the *tenor* [in the previous example, the man], and the thing used to compare is the *vehicle* [in the previous example, the snake]. In implied metaphors, they become one thing, as in this example, "Last night I plowed through a book," because the act of reading is inferred by the metaphor of "plowing through." (260)

    Because metaphors have this implied aspect, they are often abstract and embedded in language.

2. Share the following example with students to begin the discussion of how pervasive metaphors are in life as well as how they work through time and develop from numerous sources:

    > If you say someone was *sacked* (fired), you are using a term that originated from the practice of handing workmen their tool sacks upon discharging them (Rosenthal and Dardess). If you *sack* the quarterback by tackling him (or

her) behind the line of scrimmage, you're relying on a different metaphorical origin. It comes from the *sack* that means to loot and pillage, presumably because it was in sacks that one carried away the loot. And if you "hit the *sack*," you are using a World War II expression for going to bed, which for a soldier was often a bedroll or sleeping bag—a "sack" (Pugh et al. 13).

Students might consider current terms that suggest a connection to a metaphor: *periodt* (or *periot*), for example, is a term used in texts to mean the final word on a subject. Many (if not most) slang terms have metaphors at their heart. Even if students (or teachers) don't know the origin of the metaphors people commonly use—a *blanket of snow* or *bending someone's ear*—metaphors pervade the English language, and discussing this passage is a good way to begin to consider how they are used in English.

3. Have students listen carefully for several days for metaphors they hear around them. To get them started, make some suggestions of terms to listen for. Dong provides her students with a list of many uses for the word *bread* as literal, bread, but also as other ideas, as in these common sayings: knowing which side your *bread*'s buttered on; taking *bread* out of someone's mouth, and *bread* as money. Have students keep notes on what they find until the class discussion; at that time, list all they found on the board.

4. Then have students select one metaphor they want to listen for in particular—the use of a specific term such as *table* or *bread*, or transportation or sports terms used as metaphors. They should follow their selected metaphor's use through several days (or longer), noting whenever they hear the metaphor and how it was used: by whom and in what situation. After they have several encounters with the metaphor, have them report to the class about its use—its frequency and any variations in meaning or situation they found. They also might find that certain metaphors are ineffective in some situations, perhaps even inappropriate for a few situations. By

seeing metaphors used in real-life contexts, students learn about language development and its layers as well as how to more effectively use it. Dong notes that "research has shown that class discussion of metaphorical language can cultivate critical and creative thinking and language skills" (33). Investigating and reporting the metaphors they find in everyday language will benefit all students' development of language understanding.

Acquiring Academic Language

Carroll and Hasson note that some ELLs have become so proficient with the English they use in social situations that teachers may assume they have the language skill necessary to write effectively with academic language, even though the two are separate dialects. Learning to use academic language is not only a necessity for ELLs—it may also be a necessity for native English speakers, many of whom do not yet have in their linguistic toolbox the vocabulary or syntax expected for academic writing. It's highly possible that all students will need some understanding of the dialect that is academic language expected for tests.

1. Begin by collecting pieces of academic writing appropriate for your students' level to read together in class. I find that, if the piece is too long, my students become overwhelmed, so in those cases I use passages (introductions, bodies, conclusions—at different times) instead of whole texts. As students read the academic pieces, ask them to mark differences they see between what they are reading and what they might say if they were retelling the same information. Discuss what they found and make some lists of differences. Students should notice specifics that correspond to these generalities: word choice (more formal); sentence structures (more complex) and sentence length variety (less variety than in speech); and, of course, differences in content and larger structures such as paragraphs and so on.

Extending Your Knowledge

Susan Heck explains that many native English speakers, when learning academic language, exhibit aspects of second-language learners. In the same way ELLs might use vocabulary or syntax from their native language in acquiring the new language, inexperienced native speakers often transfer aspects of speech to their writing. Hagemann, also seeing similarities between learning a second language and acquiring the dialect of academic English, makes this assertion: "Whether students acquire two languages or two dialects, their success depends on their ability to develop a different mental representation for each system" ("Bridge" 76). We can help all students do that.

Have students consider why those choices might be appropriate for the situation; that is, why does academic writing often contain these characteristics? This investigation is important because it helps students understand that the language and structures of this kind of writing are useful in certain situations, but it doesn't set up academic writing as the only way to write or the only correct way to write. It's a kind of writing that fits a situation, just as informal writing fits other situations.

2. Next, ask students to notice what they already know how to do with regard to the traits of academic writing. Do they know the sentence structures they've observed? The vocabulary? The larger structures, such as topic sentences and thesis statements and integrating others' words into our own? When students first notice the differences and then compare those differences to what they know, they are ready to learn the traits that will move them closer to the kind of writing that is accepted in academic situations.

3. Finally help student begin to acquire the features of academic writing through practice in the classroom. Cruz suggests providing a scaffolded approach to learning academic English, using the language and structure of academic language orally first. Have students work together to gather information about a topic of interest to the class and present their findings in academic language. By using more formal, academic language orally first, students prepare themselves for the writing that will follow. Cruz suggests giving students sentence patterns to use in oral presentations, patterns that will transfer into writing. Her suggestions include the following:

> According to (source), (state your argument …)
> As noted by (state the occupation and name of source), (state your argument …)
> Opponents believe that …: however … (16)

The book *They Say/I Say: The Moves That Matter in Academic Writing* (Graff and Birkenstein) provides similar help that I have found beneficial for my students. It contains frames and patterns that help students integrate others' words into their own writing, in the style of academic writing, as well as sentence patterns, like those from Cruz, that help students make the moves expected in academic writing. By practicing these as a class and then individually, students begin to acquire the language patterns they need to be successful with academic language.

Language Change

Discovering Different Terms for Similar Ideas

Sometimes even native speakers are unaware that other native speakers use different terms to refer to the same item or action. I enjoy my husband's use of *tricky bars* to refer to the *jungle gym* of my childhood playground—the metal climbing bars found in many schoolyards. As we have traveled around the United States, we have noticed the prevalence of *pop* or *soda* differs when people refer to carbonated drinks.

1. Begin the lesson by asking students to share the words they have for different items or activities. Some questions I ask to get students started include the following:

    - What do you call the things we often eat for breakfast that are a batter poured on a hot pan and then turned over and served with butter and something sweet, often syrup?
    - What do you call the pan those things are cooked on?
    - What do you call the long piece of furniture people sit on in the main social room of the house?
    - What do you call that room?
    - What do you call it when the sun appears each day? When it disappears?

    When students have discussed their various answers to the questions, discuss other terms they may use that differ. For instance, many people call their grandparents by family names, rather than traditional ones. There are other regionalisms and words that change through time, too. People from older generations may have used different words for something that was in style (*groovy*, *hot*, *cool*, and so forth). Have students think of as many examples as they can. Then have students pick an idea they find interesting and conduct informal surveys about people's use of the terms for that idea. For example, they could do a study about what people call a certain thing, such as what they call carbonated drinks.

2. Next, have students report their findings and conclusions to the class: Do people from certain places use similar terms, or is the usage more a reflection of age or gender? What are students' feelings about what they learned? Helping students conduct a mini-ethnographic study of these

terms can expand their understanding of English as well as contribute to a sense of the way language develops in different areas and among different groups.

Alternative Suggestion: As an additional look at how terms are used differently, students can research the use of different language patterns by gender (e.g., the assumption that girls use more color words), or students could write a paper about a conceptual word and how it is used in different sources (see, e.g., Dean, *Strategic* 111–21).

Learning Common Words in Different Languages

One aspect of language I find interesting is the way universals are represented in different languages. I still remember a friend in elementary school who had emigrated from Sweden with her family and whose words for animal sounds were different from mine. I remember being fascinated to learn that what I thought should have been the same sound—after all, animals don't have different languages—was different for people who speak different languages. A few years ago, I watched a Public Broadcasting Service (PBS) television special about the developing brain. In the segment on babies' brains, the researchers found that all children are born with the ability to make all the sounds of all languages. By eleven months, however, their brains are wired to make the sounds of their own language. I assume, then, that we translate animal sounds into our own range of sounds.

1. As an introduction to this idea, begin class by reading two picture books that deal with common sounds or words in different languages. The book *Cock-a-Doodle Doo! What Does It Sound Like to You?* (Robinson) tells how common sounds—sneezes and animal noises, for example—sound in different languages. The book *Yum! Yuck!* (Park and Durango) tells of common exclamations in a variety of languages. Reading these with students gets them thinking about language diversity.

2. Discuss with the class the way different languages express common ideas or thoughts. Some students will know other languages and can share common expressions. If you have students with native languages other than English who are willing to share with the class, have them teach the class common expressions. For instance, they can share greetings ("Hello," "Good morning," "Goodbye"), felicitations ("Happy Birthday," "Happy New Year," and so forth), ways to show appreciation ("Cool!," "Thanks!"),

ways to show dismay or disapproval ("Oh no," "Take a hike," and so forth), or slang terms that might correspond to some that native English speakers use. This exploration of common usages in different languages can help students understand more about language in general and can generate curiosity and wonder about English in particular. Why do we express ideas the way we do?

Rhetorical Grammar

Generating Sentences with Patterns

As I mentioned earlier, learning sentence patterns can help students—both ELLs and native speakers—expand their range of expressions for different situations. Specific to this is the use of academic sentence patterns described earlier, but the concept can apply as well to other situations and other sentence types. I have a few different sentence patterns I use with students to help them generate writing at the same time as they learn some sentence patterns that may be of use to them in a variety of situations.

The first set of patterns comes from the book *I Want to Be* (Moss). In the book, a girl's response to the question about what she wants to be when she grows up isn't a traditional one (a lawyer, a teacher, a firefighter); instead, she describes characteristics in sentences that follow two different patterns.

1. Read the book to students first so they can see the concept of the book and become familiar with the patterns. Then display the patterns and have students use them to write their own "I want to be . . ." sentences, encouraging them to use vivid verbs and imagery for the nouns and adjectives. The first pattern is exemplified in the following sentences from the book:

> ### Extending Your Knowledge
>
> Cornelia Paraskevas notes that:
>
> > Pattern imitation helps writers create sentences—under careful guidance—that they would not necessarily create on their own, thus helping them expand their natural repertoire of syntactic constructions. Imitation is the first step toward giving writers choices that reflect their stylistic and rhetorical competence. (66)
>
> I agree and see that the patterns I practice with students eventually find their way into their writing.

I want to be green but not so green that I can't also be purple.
I want to be fast but not so fast that lightning seems slow.

With this pattern, I encourage students to see that the completer is not a thing, but a describer—an adjective. Following the initial assertion "I want to be [*something*]," students complete the pattern with the starter "but not so [*something*] that . . ." Although this particular pattern is used to describe, the general pattern of assertion followed by limitation is one that students can use in many situations, including academic ones. After students share the sentences they've written in this pattern, have them, as a class, consider other possible situations where this pattern might be useful. For example, students could consider a sentence such as this one: "Hamlet is indecisive, but not so indecisive that he fails to do something."

The second pattern is exemplified by the following examples:

I want to be a language, a way to share thoughts.
I want to be a new kind of earthquake, rocking the world as if it's a baby in a cradle.

With this pattern, students complete the starter with a *something*, although it's not a *something* people usually are. People are doctors and clerks and business owners, not languages or earthquakes. The assertion, then, is followed by an elaboration—either a restatement (*appositive*) or an elaboration beginning with certain kinds of words: *-ing* words (*participial phrases*) or subordinate conjunctions (modeled by other sentences in the book). With this little explanation, students are amazingly ingenious in elaborating their own sentiments and learning new patterns for sentences they can use in multiple situations. Again, follow this writing with discussion of how, although students used the pattern for a particular purpose, the pattern can work in other situations when students want to explain more about an idea in an efficient manner—not in another whole sentence. An example of this pattern for an academic essay could be the following: "Romeo in love was an optimist, believing that feuds would fail in the face of such a love."

2. Two other books can serve as models for other patterns, particularly for how to add ideas to a core sentence: *Here Is the African Savanna* and *Here Is the Tropical Rain Forest*, both by Madeleine Dunphy. In these books, Dunphy includes sentences that grow incrementally longer as the observer looks more and more closely at a scene, which is the title and first sentence of the book. Dunphy begins with an obvious feature of the place (rain or grass, in these two books) and establishes a base sentence from which all other sentences in the book grow. As the reader moves through the book,

not only do the sentences grow longer with dependent clauses, but the subject of the sentence focuses on different aspects of the scene, subordinating the previous idea, until the last sentence returns to the subject of the first sentence. For example, the first sentence in *Here Is the African Savanna* reads, "Here is the grass that grows on the plain which turns green or brown depending on rain: Here is the African savanna." The next page offers this sentence: "Here are the zebras who eat the grass that grows on the plain which turns green or brown, depending on rain: Here is the African savanna." After identifying lions, giraffes, trees, baboons, impalas, birds, hippos, and the river (among other items), the last sentence returns to the grass. To show the cumulative effect, here is the last sentence of *Here Is the Tropical Rain Forest*:

> Here is the rain that fills the river, which is home to the caiman that fights the jaguar who stalks the peccaries that eat the figs, which are dropped by the monkeys that flee from the eagle who hunts the sloth that hangs from the tree, which holds the bromeliad that shelters the frog who bathes in the rain that drizzles and pours and may fall every day in this lush and wet world: Here is the tropical rain forest.

This process of building a long sentence full of dependent clauses works best if the class practices together first. Have students think of a foundation sentence, about the classroom, perhaps. As a class, build on that sentence with dependent clauses (students don't have to know the name of the construction, but they can get the idea from the model). As the class works together, be sure to discuss what it is they are doing and why some suggestions work better than others for the sense of the sentence. Then have students start with their own idea and build their sentences by adding new subjects and subordinating previous ideas. In this way, students learn about subordination at the same time as they develop sentence sense by seeing how ideas can combine effectively.

3. A last sentence pattern I use is from *The Important Book* (Brown). In this book, Brown uses a pattern to describe several items that are familiar to young readers. The pattern identifies what the important thing is about the item and then notes several other aspects of the item before concluding with a repeat of the initial assertion about the important thing, as in this example:

> The important thing about the sky is that it is always there. It is true that it is blue, and high, and full of clouds, and made of air. But the important thing about the sky is that it is always there.

After you read the book to students, have them articulate the pattern and then use it for writing. I use the pattern with any number of topics, sometimes having students use it to write a summary for a concept I have taught or for a particular reading the students have completed. To me, the "important" thing isn't one particular aspect (a "right answer," so to speak) as much as it is that each student is able to identify what is important to them about the topic or article and use ideas in a pattern that might serve them well in other situations.

Following is the example I wrote:

> The important thing about sentence patterns is that they help students develop their sentence sense. They can also help students learn punctuation or practice language that is unfamiliar to them. They can be a place to take risks and generate writing. But the important thing about sentence patterns is that they help students develop their sentence sense.

Alternative Suggestion: The following sentence from White's *Stuart Little* could also be used to help students imitate long sentences as a way to consider how writers build sentences (even if they don't want to write sentences of this length in their own writing regularly):

> In the loveliest town of all, where the houses were white and high and the elm trees were green and higher than the houses, where the front yards were wide and pleasant and the back yards were bushy and worth finding out about, where the streets sloped down to the stream and the stream flowed quietly under the bridge, where the lawns ended in orchards and the orchards ended in fields and the fields ended in pastures and the pastures climbed the hill and disappeared over the top toward the wonderful wide sky, in this loveliest of all towns Stuart stopped to get a drink of sarsaparilla. (qtd. in Sweet 72)

Combining to Add Detail and Interest

All students can benefit from work with sentences—and sentence combining can be used to teach them a variety of structures that are useful in all the writing they do: in school, on tests, and for life. In fact, the more automatic some structures are, the better help they are to students who are writing in the constrained circumstances of tests. In the following lesson, which uses sentence combining to create appositives, students learn how to identify, punctuate, and generate appositives—all of which can be helpful preparation for large-scale tests and for writing in general.

1. Have students look at sets of sentences with the appositive structures underlined. These sentences can be pulled from the reading the class is doing (that's the best idea) or from a set you collect ahead of time, but they should represent as wide a range of appositives as your students are prepared to handle. For example, although one of my textbooks notes that any phrase that can fill a noun position (gerunds and infinitives) can act as an appositive, I usually don't include those at first as they can confuse my students. The following sentences are an example of a short sample set:

   All we had was Simon Finch, <u>a fur-trapping apothecary from Cornwall whose piety was exceeded only by his stinginess</u>. (Lee 3)

   The ruler of Florence, <u>Lorezo de'Medici</u>, asked him to deliver it as a gift to the duke of Milan. (Fritz)

   <u>A balding, smooth-faced man</u>, he could have been anywhere between forty and sixty. (Lee 166)

   An oppressive odor met us when we crossed the threshold, <u>an odor I had met many times in rain-rotted gray houses where there are coal-oil lamps, water dippers, and unbleached domestic sheets</u>. (Lee 106).

   He collected 58,000 pounds of metal—<u>tin and copper</u>—which would be heated until it was fluid. (Fritz)

   Have students examine the sample sentences, describing what they see and, in small groups, working out a definition of the underlined structures. Although, technically, the definition of an *appositive* is a noun phrase that adds information or detail, students can define it in whatever words work for them; adherence to a textbook definition isn't as important as gaining an idea of the concept. Students should notice that appositives can contain a lot more than a noun, as shown in these samples.

2. When students have an idea of what appositives do, they should also notice where they can be placed in sentences: the most common place is what some textbooks refer to as the *subject–verb split*—that is, after the initial noun in the sentence. Other placements are after any noun, at the end of the sentence, or at the beginning (probably the least common, although very interesting to construct). Have students work in pairs to investigate texts in the classroom—either ones they are reading or ones you bring in for them to use (picture books work, but so do magazines and websites)— to find more examples of sentences with appositives. By working together and discussing possible examples, students refine their understanding of the concept. In this collection process, be prepared for students to be

incorrect—that is, to gather more than appositives and to gather some of the sort I mentioned (infinitives and gerunds). Don't worry about that—the fact that students are looking for language constructions in a variety of texts outweighs an emphasis on correctness, especially at this stage of their learning. From the examples students find, select ones you will use for class work from this point on.

3. Using sentences from the examples they have collected, have students discuss the rhetorical effects of an appositive, including the effect of where it is placed: What effect does it have on the subject to interrupt the sentence and add information about it? What is the different effect of having an appositive at the beginning of a sentence rather than at the end? Do those kinds of appositives have a different effect than the ones in the middle of a sentence? Kolln explains the rhetorical effects of placement, noting that the end of the sentence is the main point of focus, but that the opening appositive can emphasize the subject. Tufte discusses different purposes for appositives that you can review with students: repeating a noun and then adding information in order to emphasize the noun; listing a number of specific examples of a general term; or using a synonym in order to explain the meaning of a term or add information about it. Students might have other ideas of their own.

4. Next, again using some of the sample sentences you or your students have gathered, have students *de-combine* sentences that contain appositives—that is, break the sentence with the appositive construction into two or more kernel sentences. For example, using one of the previous examples, I would de-combine in the following way.

> A balding, smooth-faced man, he could have been anywhere between forty and sixty. (Lee 166)

> He was a balding man.
> He had a smooth face.
> He could have been anywhere between forty and sixty.

Again, there isn't a single right answer to this practice; my students often get more kernel sentences than I do from de-combining. The point is that they begin to see how ideas from individual sentences combine into a single sentence with an appositive.

5. After students have de-combined sentences, have them trade the kernel sentences with someone who isn't familiar with the sentence and ask the student to recombine the sentences in more than one way. One sen-

tence might be similar to the original, but the other should be different. For example, recombining the previous sentence, students might write this: "With his smooth face, the balding man could have been anywhere between forty and sixty." Requiring students to combine in at least two ways pushes them to consider other constructions and allows for class discussion on the rhetorical effects of appositives—as compared with other choices writers have. Discuss the following questions: Which sentences do students like better? Why? Why should a writer choose an appositive over another construction? When might it be better to choose another construction (e.g., compound constructions or dependent clauses)?

6. Students need to know something about options for punctuating appositives before they begin to write their own. Use mentor sentences to help students consider their punctuation options and the effects of choosing one option over another. Using examples like the following, show students that they have (primarily) three punctuation choices: *commas*, *colons*, and *dashes*. Although these examples all show appositives at the end of a sentence, the punctuation options still exist for other placements: appositives in the middle of a sentence can use a pair of commas or a pair of dashes while those at the beginning almost always use a dash but sometimes use a comma as well, if the comma isn't too confusing for the reader.

> For a man who liked to ask questions, Leonardo da Vinci was born at the right time—<u>April 15, 1452</u>. (Fritz)

> Everywhere there was confusion and noise: <u>grinding gears of overheated cars and the frightening drone of German scout planes.</u> (Borden 47)

> I thought of myself as hanging in the store, <u>a mote imprisoned on a shaft of sunlight.</u> (Angelou 113)

Show students plenty of examples. After examining them, have students discuss the differing rhetorical effects of the three options: How does the dash differ from the colon in the tone it seems to suggest? Are there genres where the expectation is for one kind of punctuation more than another? Why would punctuation of appositives be related to genre expectations?

7. Students need to have practice writing appositives of their own. If they need more scaffolding, have them practice first by combining cued sentences. Such sentences can be found in a variety of textbooks—and I note some of them in Appendix A—but I also explain how to create them from texts students are reading in Chapter 3. And that is what I'd prefer teachers do. When students are ready to write their own sentences with apposi-

tives, have them write two to four sentences with the same subject, something the class has been studying (a character in a novel) or something they know well. When they have the sentences written, have them combine them into one sentence that includes an appositive. Then have them write the sentence again, moving the appositive to a different place in the sentence, if possible, to see how such a move creates a different effect. For example, the following sentences were generated about Cecile from *One Crazy Summer* (Williams-Garcia):

Cecile was a poet.
Cecile participated with the Black Panthers.
Cecile was not a traditional mother.
Cecile was arrested and told the police she had no children.

Example #1: Cecile, a poet who participated with the Black Panthers, was an untraditional mother who told the police she had no children when she was arrested.

Example #2: An untraditional mother who told the police she had no children when they arrested her, Cecile was a poet who participated with the Black Panthers.

After writing sentences with appositives over a period of time and sharing the sentences with small groups and as a class to discuss their effectiveness, have students discuss and write reflectively on how using appositives benefits their writing.

Reinforce the lessons about appositives: When students have a longer piece of writing drafted, ask them to highlight nouns in the piece of writing, particularly fairly general nouns (like *students, music, messy room,* and so forth) or terms that readers might need to know more about (such as technical terms or jargon). Then have students add appositives that provide more information about the nouns. Getting into this habit of thinking of what will help the reader and of adding information—and of using appositives to do both tasks—will help students build habits of sentence construction that will help them in tests and beyond.

Questions for Reflection

1. What are the language concerns for the tests your students have to pass? How can you address these concerns in the context of the reading and writing your students already do?

2. For the aspects of the test that can't be addressed or that aren't already in your instruction, how can you address those items in ways that connect to purposes other than practicing for the test? How can you teach language in a way that allows your students to pass the test at the same time as it opens their eyes to broader language issues and teaches them language knowledge they can use outside of the test?

3. What do you know about the ELLs in your classes? How can you learn to know them and their language better? How can you implement just one or two ideas from this chapter that will benefit the ELLs as well as the native speakers in your classes?

Putting It All Together: Building a Language-Rich Classroom

Grammar bridges the world of the living to the world of writing, reading, and speaking.

—*Harry Noden*

Seeing grammar all around us—and seeing multiple ways to bring it into our students' lives—can provide opportunities for learning that exceed expectations. Students can become engaged in learning about language without even knowing it. Integrating language—the heart of what we are about—into our classrooms makes learning in the classroom meaningful to all of life. At the same time, this approach is not without challenges. In the first place, just changing from what we've done in the past can be hard. It can be scary, wondering if we know enough, if we have the energy and the time to rethink what we have done for years, wondering what will happen if we try something that might not work at first. Besides those worries, what will our colleagues think? Administrators? Parents?

There are challenges, without a doubt. Beyond the fear of change, one challenge is that this approach doesn't lend itself easily to a scope and sequence. A comprehensive, integrated approach isn't as easily planned out—adjectives and adverbs in grade 7, phrases and clauses in grade 8. But what we've done in the past when we did have a scope and sequence didn't work. How many of us wondered why students came to us in grade 9 without understanding the least bit about subjects and verbs and complete sentences? Even when I

Extending Your Knowledge

"Grammar teaching seems to be on the way back after a period of absence, but we must make sure that it is free of the fatal weaknesses that almost killed it" (Hudson 109). A return to the teaching of grammar needs to be different from what we did in the past—even if it's a little more work.

taught students in subsequent years in junior high, during the time when we were required to teach traditional terminology in a scripted scope and sequence, students would claim they had never "had" the information before—and I was certain that I had taught lessons on it to them the year before! The teaching didn't stick. It didn't work.

Even if it's not easy, though, it is possible to frame a scope and sequence with an integrated approach. Berger suggests such a plan when she describes a different sentence construction each month of the school year. With such a plan, we can be aware of and point out to students the "sentence variation of the month" in their reading, conduct mini-lessons on writing them, and expect to see them used in polished writing. This approach could help those of us who want a little more structure to our instruction, but it shouldn't limit what we do. If I'm focused on using participial phrases but I see great examples of language variation or use of appositives, I wouldn't keep silent. A plan should still allow flexibility to address the needs of the students and the content of the class.

Without a strong scope and sequence, some teachers have told me that they worry about an integrated approach allowing them to address everything they need to cover. It's true. It's hard to be sure that we will. Sorenson addresses this concern, describing some teachers' feelings that an integrated approach is "just too hit or miss" (T5). It might be that, but it doesn't have to be. What I believe, and what I tell teachers, somewhat addresses that: If we are all doing this, if we are all considering the needs of our students and finding ways to integrate language learning in the literature we study and the writing we have them work on, students will eventually get everything they need. They might not get it in a sequential way, perhaps; and they may not get it all at once. But they will get it from immersion in thinking about language as they read and write and discuss and think. If we are all doing this, they will learn. Even if all the teachers in your school or district aren't integrating grammar, aren't making language a central part of their classes, students will still benefit from what you do. Hudson, after reviewing research on literacy instruction that includes grammar study, concludes that the positive results mean that teachers "can achieve something even by studying one small area of grammar" (106). Little bits add up. Research supports integration: what we do in our classes will accrue and benefit students' learning about language.

Because the nature of teaching grammar in the context of other work of the classrooms, in connection with the reading and writing students do, is different, we have a different preparation. We have to make language instruction match *our* class and *our* students and *our* content. And there isn't really a program we can buy or borrow that will do the work of planning that for us. A few years ago,

I attended a conference with teachers interested in teaching grammar. They were all informed by research and seemed supportive of the presentations that talked about the nature of teaching grammar effectively—in context and according to student need and development. But, when a speaker presented a prepackaged program for a sentence a week, with different tasks for the sentence on each day of the week, the teachers became ecstatic. The energy was amazing. These teachers wanted a shortcut. They hoped they could avoid some of the hard work associated with this approach. Teaching according to the needs of students and the kinds of texts they read and write can be challenging. Preparation can be a little more time-consuming. Integrating language instruction is, however, more effective. So, even if it is a little more work at the start, it's worth it.

One of the most threatening aspects of teaching grammar in context is that it requires knowing something about grammar. I know that some of the teachers I work with worry that they don't know enough about grammar, that they won't have all the answers. As a result, they don't want to address anything about language or grammar for fear a question will come up that they don't know an answer to—or, if they address language at all, they want a textbook with an answer key right there. I understand the desire for security, for keeping our ethos as teachers intact, but I also don't think it matters if we know all the answers. As I do, Donna envisions an effective language arts classroom as

> a classroom where teachers will be delighted to have questions they cannot an-
> swer, for these teachers will be trying to convey to their students, from the start,
> the secret linguists have been sitting on for at least four decades: that language
> is teasingly infinite and infinitely delightful, both in its mysteries and in the hints
> it allows us to ferret out in trying to solve them. (71)

We don't have to know everything to begin. Just being curious about language is a good place to start. We can start by paying attention to language use around us—and the internet provides a wealth of opportunities to do just that.

In fact, not knowing all the answers may be a better place to begin with our students. In addressing teaching inquiry to students, a key feature in current education, Townsend observes that we don't model inquiry when we have all the answers, that "teachers rarely ask questions of real, personal uncertainty" (113). If we don't often ask questions we don't already know the answers to, we don't model true inquiry effectively for our students. She explains inquiry as "a kind of dance: Inquirers turn to others, asking for help in moving beyond their present understandings" (112). If we have all the answers, how can we speculate or wonder with our students about language and its functions? How can we effectively model for them curiosity about the possibilities that exist for answers about language? Asking students to help find answers to their questions can be an important part of learning for our students. They learn about language—and learning.

To start, though, we don't have to know a lot. We can begin by learning a little and bringing that little bit into the classroom. We don't have to learn everything at once, or in one year totally revise all our lessons. Learning to integrate grammar into the language arts is a process, and we should allow ourselves to work through the process. Part of my comfort in knowing I don't have to know everything to begin lies in questions Strong poses:

> If exercising language is the work of a lifetime ... do most of us routinely encourage middle school and high school learners to pursue language inquiries—simple at first, then more complex—focused on questions that genuinely interest them? And do we regularly use our own language learnings, whatever they may be, as authentic live demonstrations? (8)

If using language is "the work of a lifetime," certainly learning about it is, too.

Like our students, we start with what we know (simple at first, perhaps) and add to that as we learn more—and we don't stop being intrigued and (I hope) fascinated by language. It's all around us. There's so much to find and to find interesting! Then, when we bring our interest into the classroom along with what we're also learning as we go along, we encourage students to become interested in language, in grammar. I'll admit, sometimes students have said my enthusiasm for a well-crafted sentence or an interesting use of language or a new word is "weird," but they also grow to enjoy it and bring me examples they think I'll appreciate. Recently, a student emailed me a clip of a sitcom where grammar was the center of the humor. I loved that she knew I would appreciate it. When my students do that, when they start bringing me examples of language from their world, I know they are growing attentive to how they (and others) use language. That's a start.

As teachers, we can begin with learning a little more about language than we knew last year and then apply what we learn as we learn it. I suggest starting with one unit of study and integrating language learning into that unit first. Or find one way to talk about language and integrate that. Then, the next year or semester, as you learn a little more, revise another unit or add another piece—and so on, until language learning is a part of everything you teach. Until grammar is all around you and your students in classroom.

Finding Grammar in Our World

To get grammar to surround us in the classroom, we need to find language curiosities all around us and bring them to class. I receive emails all the time—I assume other teachers do, too—about interesting aspects of the English language that my friends, rightly, assume I will find interesting. A while back, a friend sent me a list of sentences for "word lovers." Some of the sentences are these:

- A bicycle can't stand alone; it is two tired.
- Time flies like an arrow; fruit flies like a banana.
- A will is a dead giveaway.
- A calendar's days are numbered.

Bringing these sentences into class and discussing why they are humorous enough to get passed around social media, even if we don't mention the reasons (such as the difference between *like* as a verb and *like* as a preposition), can help students become curious about language, curious enough to wonder, to ask questions, and to develop sensitivity to the ways language can work for them. I don't have to know the terms for why these sentences create their effects to talk about them, but, if my students brought up the questions, I would be so thrilled that they were interested enough to notice and ask that I would go learn the reason. The point isn't just my knowing answers. The point is students increasing their awareness and curiosity about language and how it works and how it works for them.

Whenever I find something interesting about language, I collect it. Eventually, I bring it to class, and I share what I found with my students. Although these "language adventures" may not always be strictly connected to content (although many of them could be), they are useful because they tell students that my class is a place where we talk about language and wonder about how it works and what people do with it.

The meme in Figure 5.1 (see next page) is one that could come into any lesson where we are talking about adjusting language to situation. Certainly, it deals with punctuation, which we could also talk about. I use it here to show that we have access to many memes like this online that can add some interest and humor to the talk about language in our classes. This is just one from a series featured on Celadon Books' "grammar memes" webpage (Dukes).

Let's eat, Timmy.
↳ Correct at the
    dinner table

Let's eat Timmy.
↳ Correct on a raft
    in the ocean

FIGURE 5.1. One example of a language meme: Commas can be a matter of life or death and here is the proof. Remember this the next time you are lost at sea (Dukes). (Image credit: redbubble.com)

A clever satire on grammar published by *The Onion* is funny enough that it gets students interested in why the English language works the way it does, and it can develop in them interest in language's structures ("Rules Grammar Change"). Because the satirical article "announces" a governmental change in syntax and because the article follows that change, teachers and students can discuss parts of sentences as well as patterns of language (grammar!) and how these patterns help us communicate. Dave Barry wrote columns as "Mr. Language Person" that introduce, in humorous ways, many issues related to all aspects of language: punctuation, spelling, word change, usage, and so forth. Many of these "Ask Mr. Language Person" columns are available online, and they encourage conversations about the importance of usage in relation to the content and situation.

Grammar is all around us. Every day we are surrounded by it. Puns are a "generic name for those figures which make a play on words" (Corbett and Connors 399). A specific kind of wordplay traditionally called *paronomasia*, more currently called a *paragram*, changes one or more letters of a word or expression to create humor or irony, or, Collins suggests, to achieve "dramatic, critical—or bathetic—effect" (129). Thus, *Swan Lake* becomes *Swine Lake* in a Marshall book about pigs performing a ballet; a chapter on grammar in electronic communication in *Woe Is I* (O'Connor) is titled "Email Intuition"; and Lars Anderson uses a paragram in the title of a *Sports Illustrated* article about exercise programs for NASCAR pit crews with "Making a Fit Stop." Once they're aware of paragrams (and other ways to play with words), students will find them everywhere—in ads and memes and on T-shirts. Having students collect what they find and share them shows, once more, how much language—grammar!—is all around us. And, when students need what Collins refers to as "attention-catching language" (125) for titles or other writing, they have one more device they can try.

Teachers will need to pay attention to the ways words change—certainly their students will use words in new ways that teachers will have to learn as they listen and interact with their students. My husband still has trouble remembering to call our summer shoes *flip-flops* instead of *thongs*, which I constantly remind him has a very different meaning today. Anne Curzan explains how we get new words in her TED Talk, "What Makes a Word 'Real'?," which students might find interesting: we get new words because people use them!

Students might be interested in the words they use and where they came from, as many come from music or social media. A student recently told someone, when she was talking about knowing how a guy liked her, that "He just DMed me." I happened to know what it meant—but the person she was talking to did not: *direct message*, abbreviated and turned into a verb. Is it in the dictionary? Not yet, perhaps, but it may eventually get there. Words change—and nowadays, they change even faster.

Although eventually teachers should develop their own collection of language ideas and activities that connect to the specifics of their course and students, we all need a place to begin. A number of books and articles provide options for teachers to start to incorporate language exploration and discussion in their classrooms. Hudson, in trying to show what he calls the "range of things that can be done in the name of grammar," provides a list of ideas (107–8). I include a few of them here to give an idea of the possibilities teachers could implement to help students see language all around them.

- Gather examples of the use of passives in different kinds of texts and have students develop theories for the use of passives. As Hudson notes, "The immediate point is to deepen the students' understanding of grammatical conventions, but such activities also relate to general topics such as genre differences and probably help children's own use" (108).

- Look at ambiguity in jokes and consider the issue of ambiguity in other language situations. I often bring in *The Far Side* comics to talk about language; that is a way to also address humor and how language works to create it.

- Look at popular websites and consider how they use language. Students can rewrite short passages—revising direct passages to be less direct and vice versa—so that students can consider how the use of language on different sites contributes to the tone of the site and its consideration of audience.

Another source of possible classroom activities to engage language can be found in books by Richard Lederer. I use *Adventures of a Verbivore*, but his other books are also interesting, providing engaging examples of language to use as a basis for discussion. In *Adventures of a Verbivore*, chapters on slang and puns reside next to chapters on prep school language and grammar. There are several quizzes and teasers that I have used (in pieces) with my students, not for a grade but as a way to get them thinking about language and what it does and how it works and all its mysteries. One activity my students like involves sentences that can be punctuated differently to take on new meanings. The following sentence is an example: "A clever dog knows its master" (247). With an apostrophe added, the meaning is totally different: "A clever dog knows it's master" (263). Letting students play with language this way helps to create an interest in language. Also, using Truss's picture book *Eats, Shoots and Leaves: Why Commas Really Do Make a Difference!* is a way to bring pictures and language together to instigate discussion and curiosity about punctuation's relationship to meaning.

Language Exploration and Awareness (Andrews) provides numerous activities that allow students to explore language use and speculate about the meaning of their discoveries. In one exploration, students read a few articles in a tabloid newspaper and then answer questions that allow them to see how the language use makes unsuspecting readers believe the stories are 100 percent true. In other explorations, students create apologies for different people or review a number of ways to agree with someone and then consider when each is appropriate or inappropriate. These activities, and others like them, can be connected to the literature discussions the class is having or the writing students are working on. Through activities like these, students increase their awareness of language and its adaptations for different situations. After they consider these variations of language, not only are they more aware of shifting language for their own speaking and writing purposes, but they also become more sensitive to such shifts in the texts they read.

ReadWriteThink.org, a website hosted by NCTE, provides lesson plans that can also help teachers begin to build a collection of activities to bring grammar instruction into their classrooms. Table 5.1 shows a sample of the lessons that teachers might use. As the examples show, there are many ways to bring language into the classroom to help students see that grammar—in all its shapes—

is all around us and is interesting to consider. As teachers, when we've become comfortable with some of these ideas and the possibilities they represent, we should begin to find examples of our own with which to build classroom explorations or to begin class discussions. And our example of curiosity about language can encourage students to do the same and bring their own wonderings and observations to the class for exploration.

TABLE 5.1. Sample of ReadWriteThink Lessons for Integrating Grammar Instruction

Traditional Grammar		
"Manipulating Sentences to Reinforce Grammar Skills" (mini-lesson)[a]		In this lesson, students use sentences from texts they are reading to consider how to shift meaning by rearranging and shifting sentence parts.
"When I Was Young In…A Literature to Language Experience" (unit)[a]		In this lesson, students move from reading to writing as they consider and practice verb tenses.
"Playing with Prepositions through Poetry" (standard lesson)		Through writing poetry, students experiencing this lesson learn about and use prepositions.
"Action Is Character: Exploring Character Traits with Adjectives" (standard lesson)		This lesson helps students learn about effective description through listing actions and their corresponding traits (adjectives) for the characters in novels they are reading.
Editing		
"Every Punctuation Mark Matters: A Mini-Lesson on Semicolons" (mini-lesson)		This lesson teaches about semicolons by using Martin Luther King, Jr.'s "Letter from Birmingham Jail."
"What's My Subject? A Subject–Verb Agreement Mini-Lesson" (mini-lesson)[a]		This lesson uses sentences from music lyrics and news articles to explore the ways writers use subject-verb agreement to make meaning.
"The Passion of Punctuation" (unit)		Using a comparison to emoticons, this set of lessons helps students consider how punctuation can add passion and emotion to their writing.
Usage		
"Analyzing Grammar Pet Peeves" (standard lesson)		In this lesson, students explore grammar pet peeves, researching the "rules" that lead to the issues and discover attitudes about language usage.

Continued on next page

TABLE 5.1. Continued

"What Did They Say? Dialect in *The Color Purple*" (standard lesson)[a]		This lesson provides excellent strategies for introducing the concept of dialects. Students engage with recordings to explore attitudes about dialects. Although this lesson is connected to a specific novel, it can easily be adapted for any novel in which characters speak in dialects.
Language Change		
"You're the Top! Pop Culture Then and Now" (mini-lesson)		Students completing this lesson will consider *text-tapping*, looking at language through different time periods and in literature (including Shakespeare).
"Audience, Purpose, and Language Use in Electronic Messages" (mini-lesson)		In this lesson, students are encouraged to consider levels of formality among different types of communication, including digital genres.
Rhetorical Grammar		
"Style: Defining and Exploring an Author's Stylistic Choices" (standard lesson)		Although this lesson analyzes the style of Hurston's *Their Eyes Were Watching God* and stays at the analysis level, it could be used with other books, and teachers could extend the analysis into writing.
"Style-Shifting: Examining and Using Formal and Informal Language Styles" (standard lesson)		By examining their own and other writers' language use in a variety of contexts, students become more aware and therefore better able to control their language variation in different settings.
"Choosing the Best Verb: An Active and Passive Voice Mini-Lesson" (mini-lesson)		After encouraging students to explore how different genres use active and passive voice, this lesson enables them to revise their own writing for appropriate voice for the genre.

[a] Published by the International Literacy Association; all other lessons published by NCTE.

Finding Grammar in Reading

As I mentioned, integrating grammar means there isn't a traditional scope and sequence. But integrating grammar shouldn't be totally without a plan, either. We can and should make some plans—and then also allow for flexibility as questions and needs arise. Table 5.2 is an overview of what aspects of language could be taught, chapter by chapter, with *Al Capone Does My Shirts* (Choldenko). An outline like this could be designed for each piece of literature we teach. Creating this outline is not so different from the way we already plan for teaching

TABLE 5.2. Sample Outline for Teaching Grammar with *Al Capone Does My Shirts*

Chapter 1	*Rhetorical grammar*	fragments, participial phrases, lists
	Editing	dashes, compound sentences
Chapter 2	Usage	dialogue to show characters/relationships
Chapter 3	Editing	font and spelling
	Usage	names and name-calling
Chapter 4	*Rhetorical grammar*	short sentences for effect, participial phrases
Chapter 5	Usage	slang, jargon
	Traditional grammar	adverbial clauses
Chapter 6	Usage	imperatives/tone
	Editing	ellipsis
Chapter 7	Usage	politeness in language
Chapter 8	Usage	levels of formality
	Rhetorical grammar	sentence fluency to create effect
Chapter 9	*Traditional grammar*	compound sentences
Chapter 10	*Rhetorical grammar*	short sentences to create tension
Chapter 11	*Rhetorical grammar*	sentence fluency to create effect (agitation)
	Language change	connotations of words
Chapter 12	Editing	apostrophes and punctuation dialogue
	Usage	slang/nicknames
Chapter 13	*Rhetorical grammar*	effect of rhetorical questions
Chapter 15	*Rhetorical grammar*	participial phrases
Chapter 16	*Language change*	"taken to the cleaners"
Chapter 18	*Rhetorical grammar*	short sentences to create tension
Chapter 19	Usage	contrast warden's language with letter and children's
	Rhetorical grammar	lists to build imagery
Chapter 21	*Rhetorical grammar*	sentence lengths/structures to mimic what's happening
Chapter 22	Editing	colons
	Traditional grammar	adjectives
Chapter 23	Usage	dialects
Chapter 25	*Rhetorical grammar*	repetition for emphasis
Chapter 26	*Rhetorical grammar*	sentence structure to imitate moods
Chapter 27	Editing	fonts for meaning
Chapter 28	Usage	idioms
	Traditional grammar	pronouns
Chapter 30	*Traditional grammar*	compound sentences, participles for action and description
	Editing	multiple ways to punctuate compound sentences
Chapter 33	Usage	naming (and not naming)
Chapter 35	*Traditional grammar*	absolute
Chapter 36	*Traditional grammar*	compound sentences
	Rhetorical grammar	sentence structures to build tension
Chapter 37	Editing	commas (lots of different uses)
Chapter 38	*Rhetorical grammar*	sentence types for tone (simple declaratives in letter)

literature—by taking notes on the themes or characterization or literary devices that could be addressed throughout a text. Just as we do not address every literary element in a text when we study it with students, we will not address all the aspects of language that are possible, either. But knowing that they are there, that they could be addressed, will raise awareness of options. And, when we are aware of options, we can bring them in to aid in understanding the literature as well as to help students engage with language learning. In addition, it should be noted that some of the items listed in the overview are pretty brief. The study of language with reading doesn't need to take up a lot of time, so we shouldn't look at these aspects as taking time away from the study of literary elements (plot, character, theme, and so forth). In many ways, talking about language with reading should enhance the reading experience by examining how the language contributes to the literary aspect we are studying. And it should also increase students' language knowledge and curiosity.

Finding Grammar in Writing

As with reading, when we make plans to have students write specific genres, we should consider what aspects of language are characteristics as part of the writing. Certainly editing, usage, and rhetorical aspects of language are closely aligned with writing genres proficiently because genres function within social groups and respond to the social purposes of the situation. However, considering traditional grammar might also be a part of thinking about writing, and language change is an element that could relate to genres' situations and audience.

In a manner similar to the outline made for teaching a novel, teachers can outline which aspects of language they could address with a specific writing assignment. Table 5.3 shows two sample outlines. Although some of the suggestions relate to the specific characteristics of the genre, we each know our own students' needs better and, thus, could make a more appropriate outline for our classes on the more generic aspects. For instance, if students are writing movie reviews, the first outline might be aspects of language we could consider addressing as we help students work through the writing process, but, if our students need more help with commas in compound sentences, something not specific to this genre, we can adapt and add instruction for that into our plan. If students are writing a more traditional school paper, such as a literary analysis essay, the outline could look like the second example, but we could add in mini-lessons on pronoun agreement, if that is what our students need.

TABLE 5.3. Sample Outlines of Topics to Address with Two Different Writing Assignments

Outline #1: Writing a Movie Review		
	Traditional Grammar	using active verbs and adjectives effectively
	Editing	punctuating titles and proper nouns correctly
	Usage	determining the level of formality and how it's represented in the text
	Language Change	determining the jargon appropriate for the audience and movie
	Rhetorical Grammar	using appositives to condense and combine details; using subordination to show relationship between ideas
Outline #2: Writing a Literary Analysis Essay		
	Traditional Grammar	ensuring subjects and verbs agree
	Editing	punctuation and citing quoted material correctly
	Usage	identifying how academic language differs from other writing (i.e., distance, nominalizations, and so forth)
	Language Change	considering the connotations or denotations of words used in the text being analyzed as well as in the analysis
	Rhetorical Grammar	imitating sentence styles to blend others' ideas with the author's

Assessing Grammar Learning

Some teachers worry about assessing grammar instruction when grammar is integrated with reading and writing instead of in separate units that can be assessed directly. How can we measure learning when it isn't a separate unit, when it's mixed in with everything else we do, and when some of what we're teaching is more abstract than concrete? Certainly, the effect of teaching grammar with writing can be assessed through the students' writing: we can see if students are applying what they learn through the quality of their writing. Its effect on reading can be somewhat measured by students' improved reading comprehension and analysis abilities. Beyond that, however, it is also possible to assess grammar learning through attitude surveys given at the beginning and end of a course. The statements that appear in Figure 5.2, placed on continuums that range from "*totally disagree*" or "*not at all*" to "*totally agree*" or "*very much*" and administered at the beginning and end of the course, will allow us to measure students' attitude changes. The first three statements are from Hazen (182–83); the rest are my own. We can select pertinent statements from the list to use with our own classes. That selection will depend on what we will be addressing over the course of the year.

Language change is a process of decay.
Some dialects are "better" than others.
Writing and speech are essentially the same thing.
Language is an interesting subject to learn about.
Understanding sentences and how they are constructed benefits me as a reader.
Understanding sentences and how they are constructed benefits me as a writer.
Knowing about punctuation helps me read better.
Knowing about punctuation helps me write better.
I pay attention to how language changes with situations.
I talk the same way wherever I go.
People who speak with an accent are probably less intelligent.
Knowing and using good grammar is a sign of intelligence.
People shouldn't change the way they talk at home or school.
Different ways of speaking are still grammatical.
Language has power to hurt people.
People use language to manipulate ideas and emotions.
I am influenced by others' use of language.
Words mean exactly what their definitions say.
I speak a dialect.
The characters in books that use slang or dialects are not like real people.
I don't like to read books with characters that use "bad grammar."
Bad grammar is a reflection of a person's goodness.
Grammar matters in my home.
Grammar matters only at school or when we get a job.
Grammar applies only to writing.
When words change, language is weakened.
We should add new words to the dictionary every year.
Everyone in the world should be able to speak English.
Older people have a right to get upset at how younger people change the language.
English is made of words from many languages.
It's good for English to change over time.
I like to learn about language.

FIGURE 5.2. Sample statements to use for student attitude surveys.

Blending and Extending

In addition to planning aspects of language that could be addressed with the content of their classes, teachers also need to consider what else contributes to the effectiveness of an integrated language approach. The first has to do with class talk.

As is evident in the classroom dialogues I have included in this book, learning often occurs as students and teachers talk about the language that is part of their reading and writing. That means that students need to feel comfortable expressing ideas in classrooms and to respect ideas that may differ from their own. The classroom community should encourage curiosity and tolerance so that students feel confident that they can question and wonder about language. We need to help students develop the ability to tolerate ambiguity and consider ideas that may be different from their own or what they are used to. When students don't agree with others' perspectives, they should have the ability to respect the difference and maintain appropriate responses woven with those differences. In fact, using language to disagree in appropriate ways is a skill students need in abundance in today's world.

Because an important part of teaching grammar as part of content means that there will be a lot of talk in the classroom, we need to teach students how to discuss effectively. Roberts and Langer's research shows that class discussions where the teacher is the questioner and students answer back—in a kind of recitation format—isn't really a discussion. Instead, students should respond to comments made by other students and to questions posed by other students so that their engagement is real and not only a response to our questions. Discussions—the quality of classroom talk—are essential to language learning, partly because they encourage inquiry that extends beyond the classroom and partly because students are using the very substance of that inquiry: language. Our example of the kind of inquiring mind and questioning attitude that helps us learn more about language will develop students' abilities to wonder and inquire. The kinds of questions teacher pose in class will, in a large measure, determine the kinds of questions students will learn to ask—and the level of curiosity they will bring to their own language experiences outside of school. Questions should be open-ended, encouraging analysis and theorizing rather than "rightness."

We also need to be examples of curiosity and models of what it means to inquire. At one time, I wondered why signs on stores say "open" and "closed"

Extending Your Knowledge

I found that teaching grammar this way—integrated and with lots of talk—requires something different from me. As Susan Nunan states, "Before teachers of grammar can teach grammar differently, they must think differently and approach the subject analytically and pragmatically" (74). So, one of the first ways we implement an integrated approach is to adjust our own thinking in regard to teaching grammar.

instead of "opened" and "closed," which would make more sense. I theorized that English speakers must shorten some past participles. I had read that ice cream used to be "iced cream," and I saw a box in the grocery story that listed "mash potatoes" instead of "mashed potatoes." Then I saw a hut outside that advertised "shave ice" instead of "shaved ice"—so I had some other examples to bring to my theorizing. At a luncheon, I happened to be seated with a linguist, so I asked about my theory. I found out that I was partly right: English speakers do shorten past participles used this way, usually when the -ed is unheard or hard to hear (that's the part I hadn't considered). I also learned that such shortening is true of other languages as well. That's the kind of observation and questioning we should encourage in students. And, in case you don't get to have lunch with a linguist, the LINGUIST List website allows people to ask questions of linguists—so you and your students can get answers to your own questions.

Learning about language through an integrated approach requires us to be aware of different kinds of knowledge: *declarative*, *procedural*, and *conditional*. If we know about these categories, we can structure classes to allow students not only to get some information from us or from books (declarative knowledge) but also to learn how to work through problems and questions to gain procedural knowledge about language and inquiry. We know that students need to have some knowledge of how language works and how they can talk about it. However, we also need to give students time to reflect and develop conditional knowledge about language. Under what conditions do the characteristics of language take effect and how do those effects change with the situation? This question, and the reflection associated with it, could be attached to any language exploration or activity students participate in. And giving students the opportunity to think conditionally will help them transfer their learning to their lives beyond the classroom.

A Final Word—or Two

A friend standing with me in the line at a wedding reception asked what I was currently writing. I told him it was a book on teaching grammar. He made a face (a grimace, actually) and then told me the story of his school experience, especially of one junior high English teacher who taught diagramming of sentences. Although he was a reader and he generally liked English, he just didn't "get" diagramming and, consequently, did poorly in the class. "As a result," he said, "I thought I was stupid—at least in English." As I listened and thought about his story, I wondered how many other students not only miss the exciting aspect of learning about language (something they use every day and should be curious about) but also end up thinking they are stupid because they don't "get" grammar. The idea makes me sad. Language is just so fascinating!

In the end, even with a good idea like bringing language into all we do in our classrooms, success with our students isn't so much with the pedagogy as it is with us. It is, after all, our passion, our interest, and our energy that make the difference in teaching. Strong observes that "creating active learning environments resides not so much in instructional materials or in tasks themselves but rather in coaches who help students understand what they are learning, why the learning is useful, and how it might be approached" (193). As teachers, we can learn what we don't know yet—and we can answer, together and with our students, questions that arise in the context of a classroom that truly integrates grammar into the rest of the content. We can help students understand why the study of grammar matters. It just makes sense: language is part of life. How can it not be part of everything we do in an English language arts classroom?

Questions for Reflection

1. Who can you anticipate might have trouble with your using an integrated approach to grammar in your classroom? What might be their concerns? How might you help them allay these concerns?

2. What will be the first unit or area where you will integrate ideas about language into your classes? What do you need to do to plan for that integration? How will you begin to collect language items and activities that you could use?

3. In reflecting on the classroom dialogues through this book, what are some ways that the teacher could have integrated other aspects of language and grammar into this lesson? It's obvious that time has to be a consideration—we can't teach everything there is or we'd never finish a novel and we'd lose the students. What are some other considerations for what to choose to address in a classroom? How will you choose?

Appendix A

Annotated Resources

In my own growth as a learner and teacher of language, I have had many mentors—most of them authors of books and articles. When teachers ask me to recommend only one or two books to get them started, it's hard to limit myself. I have so many I could suggest—and what one teacher needs may differ from what another would find useful.

So that readers of this text might have a little more guidance than the references in this book (which is a good overall list, I think), in this appendix I offer some titles that I've annotated to give you enough information to help you make judicious selections. The titles are grouped to match the contents of the chapters of this book, to give additional places to go if the ideas of a specific chapter are of more interest to you than those of other chapters. Some of the titles are also found in my references; some are not. If I don't have a book noted in this appendix, that doesn't mean it might not help some of you. Instead, I had to be selective; these are the ones I use most often. The others in my reference list, though, are also recommended. I hope you will find the annotations useful in helping you find the resources that will best help you meet your individual needs.

Resources for Chapter 1

Traditional Grammar

For information on traditional grammar that extends beyond traditional terms and exercises, I recommend the following sources:

Crovitz, Darren, and Michelle D. Devereaux. *More Grammar to Get Things Done: Daily Lessons for Teaching Grammar in Context*. Routledge/National Council of Teachers of English, 2020.

> Lots of ideas in this book help teachers use traditional grammatical terms and concepts in meaningful ways to transfer into the daily lives of our students. And there is

a great appendix that lists different grammatical elements and the effects they tend to create. Very handy!

Hale, Constance. *Sin and Syntax: How to Craft Wickedly Effective Prose.* Broadway, 1999.

I like this book, as I mentioned in Chapter 1, because of the descriptive way Hale approaches grammar terms. Plus, the author uses actual writing to show the aspects of parts of speech and parts of sentences, so the work feels real to me, not contrived like a textbook. And an even bigger plus is the playful approach: reading this book is just plain fun.

Haussamen, Brock, with Amy Benjamin et al. *Grammar Alive! A Guide for Teachers.* National Council of Teachers of English, 2003.

This short book (about a hundred pages of text) provides twelve vignettes from classrooms to show how the ideas discussed in the chapters would look in practice. All but one of the vignettes address the different ideas of the chapters, so the book is teacher-friendly, with an interesting (and understandable) approach to grammar terms.

Editing

For work with editing, I recommend these sources:

Anderson, Jeff. *Everyday Editing: Inviting Students to Develop Skill and Craft in Writer's Workshop.* Stenhouse, 2007.

This is a very teacher-friendly book that shows how teachers can create invitations to notice, imitate, celebrate, collect, write, combine, and edit that engage students in the conventions of writing. Anderson's use of mentor sentences is masterful in this context.

Angelillo, Janet. *A Fresh Approach to Teaching Punctuation: Helping Young Writers Use Conventions with Precision and Purpose.* Scholastic, 2002.

This is another readable book about punctuation that goes beyond punctuation work with writing to include punctuation with reading, too. It provides suggestions for helping students see punctuation as a response to rhetorical effectiveness more than as rules. Students are encouraged to use mentor texts as they imitate and practice effective editing and punctuation skills. I like the author's suggestion of "accountability slips" (94) and "assistance slips" (97). Although Angelillo addresses issues from an elementary school perspective, I know some of my secondary students still had trouble with aspects of punctuation that the author gives ideas for how to teach in a more contextualized way. The ideas are adaptable.

Ehrenworth, Mary, and Vicki Vinton. *The Power of Grammar: Unconventional Approaches to the Conventions of Language.* Heinemann, 2005.

In this book, the authors show a lesson (46–48) and later in the book describe a unit with enough detail that readers can see what the teaching looked like (106–26). The rest of the book is very interesting reading and has some classroom experiences interspersed. The emphasis, however, is on grammar (especially punctuation) integrated with writing. The authors make an effective argument for the use of mentor texts for grammar instruction, but their focus is on improving writing, not necessarily improving reading (although I could see that as a consequence of their work).

Usage and Language Change

To learn more about usage, I suggest first finding a good usage book, one that addresses issues regarding usage as well as the prescriptions. For ideas on usage and language change, I've found a number of sources, but I like ones that also address teaching these issues as well as providing some background information. These two sources have been the most helpful:

Simmons, John S., and Lawrence Baines, editors. *Language Study in Middle School, High School, and Beyond: Views on Enhancing the Study of Language*. International Reading Association, 1998.

> Of the two recommended books here, this one has the most applications to teaching, with overview chapters on adolescents' study of language and contextualizing language study as well as sections on studying language through literature, using writing and speaking to study language, language use in content areas beyond language arts, and emerging trends in language study, including one chapter on film.

Wheeler, Rebecca S., editor. *Language Alive in the Classroom*. Praeger, 1999.

> Another book based on linguistic principles, this one has five sections. The first addresses the issues related to grammar instruction (particularly traditional instruction), while the second one has chapters on various linguistic applications in classrooms. The third and fourth sections deal with teaching language with writing and literature, while the last one is about dictionaries and online sources for grammar. Like the other book, the ideas are interesting and applicable to a wide range of classrooms.

Rhetorical Grammar

Books that address rhetorical grammar are more plentiful (see Chapter 2 for more ideas). For an overview, though, I'd suggest these two sources:

Kolln, Martha. *Rhetorical Grammar: Grammatical Choices, Rhetorical Effects*. 4th ed., Longman, 2003.

> This book gives a good overview of the idea of rhetorical grammar. Although there's a lot of grammar here, the text is not hard to follow, and the emphasis on the effects of grammatical choices is part of the application of grammar through the whole book.

Schuster, Edgar H. *Breaking the Rules: Liberating Writers through Innovative Grammar Instruction*. Heinemann, 2003.

> I really enjoyed this book. The writing is engaging, and the ideas are applicable to the classroom. Although Schuster doesn't provide scenarios for how the lesson ideas play out, once teachers have a vision of what integrated grammar instruction looks

like and an idea of what lessons can be found in this book, they shouldn't have any trouble adapting the ideas to the needs of their students.

Resources for Chapter 2

I could have a long list for this section; however, to be efficient, I include here three that I found particularly helpful.

Johnson, Thomas R. *A Rhetoric of Pleasure: Prose Style and Today's Composition Classroom*, Boynton/Cook, 2003.

> In this book, Johnson provides a rationale for teaching style—rhetorical grammar— to students as a way to communicate effectively and appropriately. At the same time, Johnson hopes students come to look on using language this way as pleasurable, not painful. In an appendix, Johnson provides one of the most concise summaries of rhetorical devices I've found; they're very helpful for me in learning on my own as I find structures I don't know the names for.

Killgallon, Donald. *Sentence Composing for Middle School*. Heinemann, 1997.

> This book (and its companions that have been published since) present exercises for sentence work: combining as well as imitating and generating. Although I use the sentences sometimes when I am too pressed for time to make up or find my own, I have had to be selective. Sometimes the exercises are pretty challenging. I do them first myself—just to make sure they are appropriate for my students (despite the title including "*Middle School*") and to make sure they help me accomplish the goals I want for my students. In other words—this can be a great resource, but it isn't one that teachers should use without thinking first.

Tufte, Virginia. *Artful Sentences: Syntax as Style*. Graphics, 2006.

> I *loved* this book for teaching me more of the subtleties of stylistic grammar. Lots of examples really enrich this book's value because I could use them when I wanted to teach a concept, too. It's not a book for the students, but it will help teachers feel more prepared—and then have some sentences/passages to use in instruction.

Resources for Chapter 3

I haven't found any books that specifically address using grammar or language as a way to improve students' reading. But there are some articles—and more are being published all the time now. From what I've found, I would recommend the following:

Burke, Jim. "Developing Students' Textual Intelligence through Grammar." *Voices from the Middle*, vol. 8, no. 3, Mar. 2001, pp. 56–61.

> This article explains some strategies for helping students understand how texts work—through grammar. Although there are references to writing and test preparation, some of the ideas also apply to reading more effectively.

Reid, Louann, editor. "Contexts for Teaching Grammar." *English Journal*, vol. 95, no. 5, May 2006, pp. 9–114.

> In this issue of *English Journal*, there are several articles that discuss using language as a way to improve students' reading at the same time as they develop facility with and knowledge about language. Specifically, I recommend articles by the following authors: Bonnie Warne, Eileen Simmons, and Barbara Stanford (all found in this book's Works Cited section). These articles contain additional practices that can help teachers use language to build reading proficiency.

Reid, Louann. "Teaching Grammar in Contexts *for* Writing." *Teaching Writing: Craft, Art, Genre*, by Fran Claggett with Joan Brown et al., National Council of Teachers of English, 2005, pp. 136–51.

> After a brief rationale for teaching grammar in the context of reading, Reid provides several suggestions for activities that include sentence combining, writing found poems, or adding adjectives with texts students are reading. The author ends the chapter with an overview of research about teaching grammar and writing. That chapter echoes the ideas presented in this book.

Resources for Chapter 4

There are a number of resources that address issues of preparing students for tests and teaching English language learners—but they don't focus on language. These sources do more than others.

Freeman, Yvonne S., and David E. Freeman. *Academic Language for English Language Learners and Struggling Readers: How to Help Students Succeed across Content Areas*. Heinemann, 2009.

> This book focuses on helping all students learn to use academic language. It begins with a theoretical framework but also uses a genre approach to help teachers determine difficulty levels and consider how to help students with a range of language abilities learn to use strategies for academic writing tasks.

Gilliland, Betsy, and Shannon Pella. *Beyond "Teaching to the Test": Rethinking Accountability and Assessment for English Language Learners*. National Council of Teachers of English, 2017.

> This book looks at the recommendations from the "NCTE Position Paper on the Role of English Teachers in Educating English Language Learners (ELLs)" and presents ideas for implementing those recommendations (National Council of Teachers of English). It uses a genre-based approach to help ELLs learn as well as be prepared for tests.

National Council of Teachers of English. "English Language Learners." *Resources*, ncte.org/resources/english-language-learners.

> This site contains links to articles, books, and lesson plans that teachers can use to design instructional practice appropriate for ELLs in their classes.

Resources for Chapter 5

For ideas about finding grammar—language—all around you and for integrating it smoothly into your curriculum, these are sources I recommend.

Andrews, Larry. *Language Exploration and Awareness: A Resource Book for Teachers.* 3rd ed., Erlbaum, 2006.

> This book presents numerous interesting activities (what Andrews calls "explorations") that develop in students an interest, knowledge, and curiosity about language. For example, one activity asks students to keep a log of the fillers they hear people use in conversation and generalize about the function of fillers in speech. The activities are definitely doable and accomplish the purpose of engaging students in wide exploration of many aspects of language, including spelling, dialects, and semantics as well as word meanings and speech.

Crovitz, Darren, and Michelle D. Devereaux. *Grammar to Get Things Done: A Practical Guide for Teachers Grounded in Real-World Usage.* Routledge/National Council of Teachers of English, 2016.

> This book uses as its premise that the best way to get students engaged with language is to help them see it in the world around them and to use it to do things in the real world. The authors present lots of practical ideas with plenty of directions and details for teachers to know how to implement the suggested lessons.

Appendix B

A Brief Note about Foundational Grammar Knowledge

Some readers might want to know what rules and definitions form a basic knowledge of grammar for teachers. I don't think I can give rules or definitions. As Schuster (*Breaking*) argues effectively, they often don't work. I will be frank and say that I learned, mostly, from teaching my students out of their eighth- and ninth-grade textbooks. So, I learned the rules and definitions first. Then, as I helped students work through the activities we engaged in, I found myself thinking more and more about the ways the definitions and rules didn't work; as a result, I had to learn more, ask questions, read, expand on what our book said, and allow students to modify what we used to explain ourselves. So, what follows is my own way of explaining what I think, at the start, a teacher should know.

Parts of Speech

Although I hesitate to put too much emphasis on this, teachers should probably have a sense of what constitutes the concepts of nouns, verbs, adjectives, adverbs, prepositions, conjunctions, and pronouns. Teachers can consider forms as part of understanding parts of speech rather than definitions:

- *Verbs* can have *to* in front of them and may change form for past, present, or future time.
- *Nouns* take a determiner: *a, an, the.*
- *Prepositions* show relationships and come at the beginning of a group of words.

Once teachers have an understanding of the parts of speech, they should think about issues related to traditional explanations. Have students play around to figure out what we mean by parts of speech. For instance, I help students see that a word doesn't belong to only one part of speech by having them think of one word that could be multiple parts of speech. My students see that *dog* might usually be a noun, but it can also be an adjective (*dog*house) or, with changes in form, it could be a verb (to *dog* someone) or an adverb (*doggedly*). I have them write stories with no pronouns so that they come to see the value of having shortcuts in language—but also the problem if we don't have a clear referent for a pronoun. What I'm trying to say is that this knowledge of parts of speech isn't about definitions so much as it is about concepts. Understanding parts of speech gives me and my students a vocabulary to talk about language—when we read and write and speak.

Terms

Students need to be familiar with some terms in order for me to talk to them about their writing—both about the problems they have and the ways they could be more effective. So teachers should know these concepts as well. These terms include *phrase* and *clause*. A *phrase* is a group of words that go together. The group might have a noun or a verb, or even something that looks like both, but not as subjects and predicates, not in the sense of a sentence (see how hard it is to define?). Some types of phrases I might address are these:

- prepositional phrase
- noun phrase
- verb phrase
- verbal phrases—infinitive, gerund, and participial

A *clause* is a group of words with both a subject and a predicate. Some types of clauses I might address are these:

- *Dependent/subordinate*—although I sometimes address different kinds of clauses (adjective, adverb, and noun), I generally don't get too specific. We do talk about clauses as part of sentence structure (understanding ineffective fragments, for instance, requires an understanding of dependent clauses) and as part of style (e.g., moving adverbial clauses around).
- *Independent*—if students have trouble with sentence boundaries, an understanding of "stand-alone" clauses is essential.

After I explain, as best as I can, the difference between phrases and clauses, I give examples and then I play "Thumbs" with my students: I take a well-known text and break it up into phrases and clauses listed on an overhead transparency. Then, as I show the group of words, one at a time, my students put their thumbs up if it's a phrase and their thumbs down if it's a clause. For example, one year I used the poem "'Twas the Night before Christmas" (Moore) just before the winter break. "All through the house?" A phrase—thumbs up. "Not a creature was stirring?" A clause—thumbs down. I vary the way I break up the text so that students don't think clauses are long and phrases are short—so that they really have to look at them and get a sense of them. Repeating this activity, or one like it, usually gets my students to understand phrases and clauses as well as they need to for our work in class. The knowledge is reinforced by my referring to phrases and clauses when we read and write.

Sentence Structure

I learned most about sentence structure from diagramming—but I know that it doesn't help most people learn about sentences. No matter how teachers learn about sentence structure, they should pay attention to sentences, to how they work and how writers use them. I sometimes teach my students about simple, compound, complex, and compound–complex sentences. I have a simple process they follow: looking first for coordinate conjunctions and checking to see if they join "whole sentences" (if they find them, the sentence is either compound or compound–complex) and then looking for subordinate conjunctions and checking to see if they are acting as starts to clauses or phrases (if they start clauses, the sentence is either complex or compound–complex). Process of elimination determines the answer. With the conjunctions listed on posters on the walls, students can follow the quick process and identify most sentences. Knowing something about these types and about how sentences are structured allows teachers to address correctness issues as well as rhetorical issues (style) and sentence effectiveness.

The rest of what I come to know comes from the needs of my students and my own interest. I see sentences with structures I find interesting, so I look up the pattern in a book and find out its name: *appositives, participial phrases, polysyndeton, anaphora,* and so forth. I read a grammar rant about how language is used, so I look up usage issues: *shall* versus *will, continuously* versus *continually, hopefully,* and so forth. I find a person's use of language noticeable in a particular situation, so I research levels of formality and bring it to the classroom talk on language. I see a sign with a play on words, so I go through my grammar books until I find a name for it: *paragram.* Each new thing I learn, each interesting example of language I hear or see around me—all of it becomes part of what I bring to the classroom. And each year what I am able to bring is more than the year before.

Works Cited

The Adventure of English, presented by Melvin Bragg. *YouTube,* uploaded by Robin C. Carter, 27 Sep. 2015, www.youtube.com/playlist?list=PLbBvyau8q9v4hcgNYBp4L CyhMHSyq-lhe.

Alvarez, Julia. "Ten of My Writing Commandments." *English Journal,* vol. 88, no. 2, Nov. 1998, pp. 36–41.

Anderson, Jeff. *Everyday Editing: Inviting Students to Develop Skill and Craft in Writer's Workshop.* Stenhouse, 2007.

Anderson, Jeff, and Deborah Dean. *Revision Decisions: Talking through Sentences and Beyond.* Stenhouse, 2014.

Anderson, Lars. "Making a Fit Stop." *Sports Illustrated,* vol. 103, no. 32, 29 Aug. 2005, p. 32.

Andrews, Larry. *Language Exploration and Awareness: A Resource Book for Teachers.* 3rd ed., Erlbaum, 2006.

Angelillo, Janet. *A Fresh Approach to Teaching Punctuation: Helping Young Writers Use Conventions with Precision and Purpose.* Scholastic, 2002.

Atwell, Nancie. *Lessons That Change Writers.* Heinemann, 2002.

Barry, Dave. "What Is and Ain't Grammatical." *Dave Barry's Bad Habits: A 100% Fact-Free Book,* by Barry, Owl Books, 1993, pp. 191–93.

Battistella, Edwin. "The Persistence of Traditional Grammar." *Language Alive in the Classroom,* edited by Rebecca S. Wheeler, Praeger, 1999, pp. 13–21.

Beers, Kylene. "Contextualizing Grammar." *Voices from the Middle,* vol. 8, no. 3, Mar. 2001, p. 4.

Benjamin, Amy. "Grammar Teaches Literature." *Syntax in the Schools,* vol. 20, no. 2, 2004, pp. 2–5.

Berger, Joan. "Transforming Writers through Grammar Study." *English Journal,* vol. 95, no. 5, May 2006, pp. 53–59.

Birch, Barbara M. *Learning and Teaching English Grammar, K–12.* Pearson Education, 2005.

Bomer, Randy. "Reading with the Mind's Ear: Listening to Text as a Mental Action." *Journal of Adolescent and Adult Literacy,* vol. 49, no. 6, 2006, pp. 524–35.

Borsheim-Black, Carlin, and Sophia T. Sarigianides. *Letting Go of Literary Whiteness: Antiracist Literature Instruction for White Students*. Teachers College Press, 2019.

Braddock, Richard, et al. *Research in Written Composition*. National Council of Teachers of English, 1963.

Bresler, Ken. "Playing the Synonym Game." *Vocabula Bound: Outbursts, Insights, Explanations, and Oddities*, edited by Robert H. Fiske, Marion Street Press, 2004, pp. 67–71.

Bryson, Bill. *The Mother Tongue: English and How It Got That Way*. William Morrow, 1990.

Burke, Jim. "Developing Students' Textual Intelligence through Grammar." *Voices from the Middle*, vol. 8, no. 3, Mar. 2001, pp. 56–61.

———. "Learning the Language of Academic Study." *Voices from the Middle*, vol. 11, no. 4, May 2004, pp. 37–42.

California Department of Education. Released test questions, "Grade 9 English–Language Arts," California Standards Test, 2008, d1h00kd22lgwsm.cloudfront.net/api/file/P4oEO5RPS9iiNDnoJH8j.

Canby, Henry S. "Preface." *An A.B.C. of English Usage*, edited by Henry A. Treble and George H. Vallins, Clarendon Press, 1937, pp. 5–9.

Carroll, Pamela Sissi, and Deborah J. Hasson. "Helping ELLs Look at Stories through Literary Lenses." *Voices from the Middle*, vol. 11, no. 4, May 2004, pp. 20–26.

Christy, Janice. *Helping English Language Learners in the English and Language Arts Classroom*, Glencoe/McGraw-Hill, 2005. Accessed 13 Aug. 2021.

Collins, Valerie. "Words of a Feather." *Vocabula Bound: Outbursts, Insights, Explanations, and Oddities*, edited by Robert H. Fiske, Marion Street Press, 2004, pp. 125–32.

Corbett, Edward P. J., and Robert J. Connors. *Classical Rhetoric for the Modern Student*. 4th ed., Oxford UP, 1999.

Crovitz, Darren, and Michelle D. Devereaux. *Grammar to Get Things Done: A Practical Guide for Teachers Anchored in Real-World Usage*. Routledge/National Council of Teachers of English, 2017.

———. *More Grammar to Get Things Done: Daily Lessons for Teaching Grammar in Context*. Routledge/National Council of Teachers of English, 2020.

Cruz, Mary C. "Can English Language Learners Acquire Academic English?" *English Journal*, vol. 93, no. 4, Mar. 2004, pp. 14–17.

Crystal, David. *The Stories of English*. Overlook Press, 2004.

Curzan, Anne. "Spelling Stories: A Way to Teach the History of English." *Language in the Schools: Integrating Linguistic Knowledge into K–12 Teaching*, edited by Kristin Denham and Anne Lobeck, Routledge, 2005, pp. 139–48.

———. "What Makes a Word 'Real'?" *TED*, Mar. 2014, www.ted.com/talks/anne_curzan_what_makes_a_word_real/transcript. Transcript.

Curzan, Anne, and Michael Adams. *How English Works: A Linguistic Introduction*. Pearson Education, 2006.

Dean, Deborah. "Framing Texts: New Strategies for Student Writers," *Voices from the Middle*, vol. 11, no. 2, Dec. 2003, pp. 32–35.

———. "Going Public: Letters to the World." *Voices from the Middle*, vol. 8, no. 1, Sep. 2000, pp. 42–47.

———. *Strategic Writing: The Writing Process and Beyond in Secondary Schools*. National Council of Teachers of English, 2017.

———. "Underground, Out the Door, in Disguise: Teaching Grammar after 1963." *English Record*, vol. 52, no. 2, 2002, pp. 27–35.

Denham, Kristin. "Teaching Students about Language Change, Language Endangerment, and Language Death." *Language in the Schools: Integrating Linguistic Knowledge into K–12 Teaching*, edited by Kristin Denham and Anne Lobeck, Routledge, 2005, pp. 149–60.

Denham, Kristin, and Anne Lobeck, editors. *Language in the Schools: Integrating Linguistic Knowledge into K–12 Teaching*. Routledge, 2005.

Devereaux, Michelle D., and Darren Crovitz. "Power Play: From Grammar to Language Study." *English Journal*, vol. 107, no. 3, Jan. 2019, pp. 19–25.

di Gennaro, Kristen, and Irene Schultz. "Style-Shifting: Examining and Using Formal and Informal Language Styles." *National Council of Teachers of English*, www.read writethink.org/classroom-resources/lesson-plans/style-shifting-examining-using. Accessed 28 Sep. 2021.

Dillard, Annie. *The Writing Life*. Harper and Row, 1989.

Dong, Yu Ren. "Don't Keep Them in the Dark! Teaching Metaphors to English Language Learners." *English Journal*, vol. 93, no. 4, Mar. 2004, pp. 29–35.

Doniger, Paul. "Shakespeare through Grammar." *Syntax in the Schools*, vol. 20, no. 2, 2004, pp. 6–11.

Donna, Jeannine M. "Linguistics is for Kids." *Language Alive in the Classroom*, edited by Rebecca S. Wheeler, Praeger, 1999, pp. 67–80.

Dukes, Jessica. "13 Hilarious Grammar Memes That Describe How We Really Feel."

Dunn, Patricia A., and Kenneth Lindblom. "Developing Savvy Writers by Analyzing Grammar Rants." *Language in the Schools: Integrating Linguistic Knowledge into K–12 Teaching*, edited by Kristin Denham and Anne Lobeck, Routledge, 2005, pp. 191–207.

———. *Grammar Rants: How a Backstage Tour of Writing Complaints Can Help Students Make Informed, Savvy Choices about their Writing*. Heinemann, 2011.

———. "Why Revitalize Grammar?" *English Journal*, vol. 92, no. 3, Jan. 2003, pp. 43–50.

Ehrenworth, Mary "Grammar—Comma—A New Beginning." *English Journal*, vol. 92, no. 3, Jan. 2003, pp. 90–96.

Ehrenworth, Mary, and Vicki Vinton. *The Power of Grammar: Unconventional Approaches to the Conventions of Language*. Heinemann, 2005.

Fagan, Barbara. "Scaffolds to Help ELL Readers." *Voices from the Middle*, vol. 11, no. 1, Sep. 2003, pp. 38–42.

Faigley, Lester. *The Brief Penguin Handbook*. 2nd ed., Pearson Education, 2005.

Francis, W. Nelson. "Revolution in Grammar." *Quarterly Journal of Speech*, vol. 40, no. 3, 1954, pp. 299–312.

Fravel, L. A. "The Role of Talk in the Refinement of Writing: Positive Effects that Accrue to Both Native Speakers and English Language Learners." *Virginia English Bulletin*, vol. 55, no. 1, 2005, pp. 67–76.

Fuchs, Hildegard. "Fantasy Objects." *Ideas Plus: Book Nine*, edited by Jane. M. Curran and Michelle S. Johlas, National Council of Teachers of English, 1991, p. 57.

Gardner, Traci. "Picture Books as Framing Texts: Research Paper Strategies for Struggling Writers." *ReadWriteThink*, National Council of Teachers of English, www.read writethink.org/classroom-resources/lesson-plans/picture-books-framing-texts.

Gates, Henry L., Jr. "Afterword." *Their Eyes Were Watching God*, by Zora Neale Hurston, Perennial, 1998, pp. 195–205.

Gold, David. "But When Do You Teach Grammar? Allaying Community Concerns about Pedagogy." *English Journal*, vol. 95, no. 6, Jul. 2006, pp. 42–47.

Graff, Gerald, and Cathy Birkenstein. *They Say/I Say: The Moves That Matter in Academic Writing*. W. W. Norton, 2006.

Graham, Steve, and Dolores Perin. *Writing Next: Effective Strategies to Improve Writing of Adolescents in Middle and High Schools—A Report to Carnegie Corporation of New York*. Alliance for Excellent Education, 2007, www.all4ed.org/files/WritingNext.pdf.

Gray, Ronald. "Grammar Correction in ESL/EFL Writing Classes May Not Be Effective." *The Internet TESL Journal*, vol. 10, no. 11, 2004, iteslj.org/Techniques/Gray-Writing Correction.html.

Grinage, Justin. "Combating Huck Finn's Censorship: A Step-by-Step Guide to Discussing the N-Word in the Classroom." *Talking About Race: Alleviating the Fear*, edited by Steve Grineski et al., Stylus, 2013, pp. 137–48.

Hagemann, Julie A. "Balancing Content and Form in the Writing Workshop." *English Journal*, vol. 92, no. 3, Jan. 2003, pp. 73–79.

———. "Bridge from Home to School: Helping Working Class Students Acquire School Literacy." *English Journal*, vol. 90, no. 4, Mar. 2001, pp. 74–81.

———. *Teaching Grammar: A Reader and Workbook*. Allyn and Bacon, 1999.

Hale, Constance. *Sin and Syntax: How to Craft Wickedly Effective Prose*. Broadway, 2006.

Harmon, Mary R., and Marilyn J. Wilson. *Beyond Grammar: Language, Power, and the Classroom*. Erlbaum, 2006.

Hartwell, Patrick. "Grammar, Grammars, and the Teaching of Grammar." *College English*, vol. 47, no. 2, Feb. 1985, pp. 105–27.

Haussamen, Brock, with Amy Benjamin et al. *Grammar Alive! A Guide for Teachers*. National Council of Teachers of English, 2003.

Hazen, Kirk. "English LIVEs: Language In Variation Exercises for Today's Classroom." *Language in the Schools: Integrating Linguistic Knowledge into K–12 Teaching*, edited by Kristin Denham and Anne Lobeck, Routledge, 2005, pp. 181–89.

Heck, Susan K. "Writing Standard English IS Acquiring a Second Language." *Language Alive in the Classroom*, edited by Rebecca S. Wheeler, Praeger, 1999, pp. 115–20.

Hillocks, George, Jr. *Research on Written Composition: New Directions for Teaching*. National Council of Teachers of English, 1986.

Hillocks, George, Jr., and Michael W. Smith. "Grammars and Literacy Learning." *Handbook of Research on the Teaching of English Language Arts*, edited by James Flood et al., 2nd ed., Erlbaum, 2003.

Horning, Ann. *Teaching Writing as a Second Language*. Southern Illinois UP, 1987.

Hudson, Richard. "Grammar Teaching is Dead—NOT!" *Language Alive in the Classroom*, edited by Rebecca S. Wheeler, Praeger, 1999, pp. 101–12.

Iyer, Pico. "In Praise of the Humble Comma." *The Eloquent Essay: An Anthology of Classic and Creative Nonfiction*, edited by John Loughery, Persea, 2000, pp. 93–96.

Johnson, Thomas R. *A Rhetoric of Pleasure: Prose Style and Today's Composition Classroom*. Boynton/Cook, 2003.

Keely, Karen A. "Dangerous Words: Recognizing the Power of Language by Researching Derogatory Terms." *English Journal*, vol. 100, no. 4, Mar. 2011, pp. 55–60.

Kennedy, John F. "Inaugural Address." *Classical Rhetoric for the Modern Student*, edited by Edward P. J. Corbett and Robert J. Connor, 4th ed., Oxford UP, 1999, pp. 459–61.

Kennedy, Randall. *Nigger: The Strange Career of a Troublesome Word*. Vintage, 2008.

Killgallon, Donald. *Sentence Composing for Middle School*. Heinemann, 1997.

Kolln, Martha. *Rhetorical Grammar: Grammatical Choices, Rhetorical Effects*. 4th ed., Longman, 2003.

Kooy, Mary, and Annette Chiu. "Language, Literature, and Learning in the ESL Classroom." *English Journal*, vol. 88, no. 2, Nov. 1998, pp. 78–84.

Kress, Gunther, and Theo van Leeuwen. *Reading Images: The Grammar of Visual Design*. Routledge, 1998.

Lederer, Richard. *Adventures of a Verbivore*. Pocket, 1994.

Lee, Jin S. "Embracing Diversity through the Understanding of Pragmatics." *Language in the Schools: Integrating Linguistic Knowledge into K–12 Teaching*, edited by Kristin Denham and Anne Lobeck, Routledge, 2005, pp. 17–27.

Loewen, Shawn. "Grammar Correction in ESL Student Writing: How Effective Is It?" *Schuylkill*, vol. 2, no. 1, fall 1998, www.temple.edu/gradmag/fall98/loewen.htm.

Lyiscott, Jamila. "3 Ways to Speak English." *TED*, Feb. 2014, www.ted.com/talks/jamila_lyiscott_3_ways_to_speak_english?language=en.

Marchetti, Allison, and Rebecca O'Dell. *Writing with Mentors: How to Reach Every Writer in the Room Using Current, Engaging Mentor Texts*. Heinemann, 2015.

Massey, Lance. "On the Richness of Grammar as an Analytical Lens in the Integrated Language Arts." *English Journal*, vol. 100, no. 4, Mar. 2011, pp. 66–70.

McDougal, Littell English. Teacher's ed., 1989.

McQuain, Jeffrey, and Stanley Malless. *Coined By Shakespeare: Words and Meanings First Penned by the Bard*. Merriam-Webster, 1998.

McWhorter, John. *The Power of Babel: A Natural History of Language*. Henry Holt, 2001.

———. *Words on the Move: Why English Won't—and Can't Sit Still (Like, Literally)*. Picador, 2016.

Meyer, Jim. "Living with Competing Goals: State Frameworks vs. Understanding of Linguistics." *English Journal*, vol. 92, no. 3, Jan. 2003, pp. 38–42.

Micciche, Laura R. "Making a Case for Rhetorical Grammar." *College Composition and Communication*, vol. 55, no. 4, 2004, pp. 716–37.

Milroy, James, and Lesley Milroy. *Authority in Language: Investigating Language Prescription and Standardization*. 2nd ed., Routledge, 1991.

Mitchell, Corey. "The Nation's English-Learner Population Has Surged: 3 Things to Know." *EducationWeek*, 18 Feb. 2020, www.edweek.org/leadership/the-nations-english-learner-population-has-surged-3-things-to-know/2020/02.

Mitchell, Koritha. "The N-word in the classroom: Just say NO." *C19 Podcast*, season 2, episode 6, Society of Nineteenth-Century Americanists, 2019, soundcloud.com/c19podcast/nword.

Murfin, Ross, and Supriya Ray. *The Bedford Glossary of Critical and Literary Terms*. 2nd ed., Bedford/St. Martin's, 2003.

Myers, Marshall. "Book Review: *Artful Sentences: Syntax as Style*." *ATEG Journal*, vol. 22, no. 1, 2006, pp. 17–18.

Myhill, Debra, et al. "Playful Explicitness with Grammar: A Pedagogy for Writing." *Literacy*, vol. 47, no. 2, 2013, pp. 103–11.

Napoli, Donna J. "Linguistics as a Tool in Teaching Fiction Writing." *Language in the Schools: Integrating Linguistic Knowledge into K–12 Teaching*, edited by Kristin Denham and Anne Lobeck, Routledge, 2005, pp. 209–21.

National Council of Teachers of English. "English Language Learners." *Resources*, ncte.org/resources/english-language-learners.

National Council of Teachers of English. "NCTE Position Paper on the Role of English Teachers in Educating English Language Learners (ELLs)." *Position Statements*, 6 Mar. 2020, ncte.org/statement/teaching-english-ells.

National Livestock and Meat Board. "United We Steak." *Beef. It's What For Dinner*, 29 Jun. 2020, www.multivu.com/players/English/8719951-beef-its-whats-for-dinner-united-we-steak.

"NCTE/IRA Standards for the English Language Arts." 1996. National Council of Teachers of English and International Reading Association, 2012, ncte.org/resources/standards/ncte-ira-standards-for-the-english-language-arts.

Nilsen, Allene Pace, and Don L. F. Nilsen. "Working under Lucky Stars: Language Lessons for Multilingual Classrooms." *Voices from the Middle*, vol. 11, no. 4, May 2004, pp. 27–32.

Noden, Harry. *Image Grammar: Using Grammatical Structures to Teach Writing*. Boynton/Cook, 1999.

Noguchi, Rei R. *Grammar and the Teaching of Writing: Limits and Possibilities*. National Council of Teachers of English, 1991.

———. "Rethinking the Teaching of Grammar." *English Record*, vol. 52, no. 2, 2002, pp. 22–26.

Nunan, Susan Losee. "Forgiving Ourselves and Forging Ahead: Teaching Grammar in a New Millennium." *English Journal*, vol. 94, no. 4, Mar. 2005, pp. 70–75.

O'Conner, Patricia T. *Woe Is I: The Grammarphobe's Guide to Better English in Plain English*. Riverhead Books, 2003.

Oxford English Dictionary. Oxford UP, www.oed.com.

Paraskevas, Cornelia. "Grammar Apprenticeship." *English Journal*, vol. 95, no. 5, May 2006, pp. 65–70.

Parkes, Malcolm B. *Pause and Effect: An Introduction to the History of Punctuation in the West*. U of California P, 1993.

Penha, James. "Teacher to Teacher: What Is Your Most Compelling Reason for Teaching Grammar?" *English Journal*, vol. 95, no. 5, May 2006, pp. 18–21.

Perrin, Robert. "Words, Words, Words: Helping Students Discover the Power of Language." *English Journal*, vol. 96, no. 5, Jan. 2007, pp. 36–39.

Petit, Angela. "The Stylish Semicolon: Teaching Punctuation as Rhetorical Choice." *English Journal*, vol. 92, no. 3, Jan. 2003, pp. 66–72.

Pollio, Howard R., et al. *Psychology and the Poetics of Growth: Figurative Language in Psychology, Psychotherapy, and Education*. Erlbaum, 1977.

Postman, Neil. *The End of Education: Redefining the Value of School*. Vintage, 1995.

Poth, Joseph. "Nontraditional Grammar and Learning Transfer." *ATEG Journal*, vol. 21, no. 2, 2006, pp. 11–13.

Pugh, Sharon L., et al. *Metaphorical Ways of Knowing: The Imaginative Nature of Thought and Expression*. National Council of Teachers of English, 1997.

Raub, Albert N. *Lessons in English: A Practical Course of Language Lessons and Elementary Grammar*. Porter and Coates, 1880.

Ray, Katie Wood. *Study Driven: A Framework for Planning Units of Study in the Writing Workshop*. Heinemann, 2006.

———. *Wondrous Words: Writers and Writing in the Elementary Classroom*. National Council of Teachers of English, 1999.

Reid, Louann, editor. "Contexts for Teaching Grammar." *English Journal*, vol. 95, no. 5, May 2006, pp. 9–114.

———. "Teaching Grammar in Contexts for Writing." *Teaching Writing: Craft, Art, Genre*, by Fran Claggett with Joan Brown et al., National Council of Teachers of English, 2005, pp. 136–51.

Roberts, Doralyn R., and Judith A. Langer. *Supporting the Process of Literary Understanding: Analysis of a Classroom Discussion.* National Research Center on English Learning and Achievement, 2000.

Romano, Tom. *Crafting Authentic Voice.* Heinemann, 2004.

Rosenthal, Peggy, and George Dardess. *Every Cliché in the Book.* Illustrated by Peter LaVigna, William Morrow, 1987.

"Rules Grammar Change." *The Onion*, Mar. 12 1997, www.theonion.com/rules-grammar-change-1819564233.

Sanders, Ella F. *Lost in Translation: An Illustrated Compendium of Untranslatable Words from Around the World.* Ten Speed Press, 2016.

"San Francisco Pushes to Rebrand 'Convicted Felons' As 'Formerly Incarcerated Person,' Drop Other Criminal Justice Language." *ABC7*, 23 Aug. 2019, abc7.com/politics/sf-pushes-to-rebrand-crime-language-drop-terms-like-felon-and-addict/5488088.

Schuster, Edgar H. *Breaking the Rules: Liberating Writers through Innovative Grammar Instruction.* Heinemann, 2003.

———. "A Fresh Look at Sentence Fragments." *English Journal*, vol. 95, no. 5, May 2006, pp. 78–83.

Shafer, Gregory. "Standard English and the Migrant Community." *English Journal*, vol. 90, no. 4, Mar. 2001, pp. 37–43.

Simmons, Eileen. "The Grammars of Reading." *English Journal*, vol. 95, no. 5, May 2006, pp. 48–52.

Smoot, Scott W. "An Experiment in Teaching Grammar in Context." *Voices from the Middle*, vol. 8, no. 3, Mar. 2001, pp. 34–42.

Sorenson, S. "What Is Integrated Language Arts?" *Literature: World Masterpieces*, edited by Roger Babusci et al., annotated teacher's ed., 4th ed., Prentice Hall, 1996, pp. T3–T5.

"Standard English." *Wikipedia*, en.wikipedia.org/wiki/Standard_English. Accessed 29 Sep. 2021.

Stanford, Barbara. "'Somebody Died?' Using Grammar to Construct Meaning in Adolescent Literature." *English Journal*, vol. 95, no. 5, May 2006, pp 60–64.

Strong, William. *Coaching Writing: The Power of Guided Practice.* Heinemann, 2001.

Tan, Amy. "Mother Tongue." *The Eloquent Essay; An Anthology of Classic and Creative Nonfiction*, edited by John Loughery, Persea, 2000, pp. 112–19.

Townsend, Jane S. "Language Arts: Explore, Create, Discover through Inquiry." *Integrating Inquiry across the Curriculum*, edited by Richard H. Audet and Linda K. Jordan, Corwin, 2005, pp. 111–35.

Truss, Lynn. *Eats, Shoots and Leaves: Why, Commas Really Do Make a Difference!* Putnam, 2006.

———. *Eats, Shoots and Leaves: The Zero Tolerance Approach to Punctuation.* Gotham, 2003.

Tufte, Virginia. *Artful Sentences: Syntax as Style.* Graphics Press, 2006.

Ullman, Tomer. "BAHFest 2013—Tomer Ullman: The Crying Game." *YouTube*, uploaded by BAHFest, 28 Jan. 2014, www.youtube.com/watch?v=Zm-sQnazFAQ.

Umbach, David B. "Grammar, Tradition, and the Living Language." *Language Alive in the Classroom*, edited by Rebecca S. Wheeler, Praeger, 1999, pp. 3–11.

Wallace, Ray. "Introduction: Reexamining the Place of Grammar in Writing Instruction." *The Place of Grammar in Writing Instruction: Past, Present, Future*, edited by Susan M. Hunter and Ray Wallace, Heinemann, 1995, pp. 1–5.

Warne, Bonnie M. "Teaching Conventions in a State-Mandated Testing Context." *English Journal*, vol. 95, no. 5, May 2006, pp 22–27.

Weaver, Constance. *The Grammar Plan Book: A Guide to Smart Teaching*. Heinemann, 2007.

———. *Teaching Grammar in Context*. Boynton/Cook, 1996.

———. "Teaching Grammar in the Context of Writing." *English Journal*, vol. 85, no. 7, Nov. 1996, pp. 15–23.

Wheeler, Rebecca S., editor. *Language Alive in the Classroom*. Praeger, 1999.

Wheeler, Rebecca S., and Rachel Swords. *Code-Switching: Teaching Standard English in Urban Classrooms*. National Council of Teachers of English, 2006.

Wiesel, Elie. "Why I Write: Making No Become Yes." *The Essay Connection: Readings for Writers*, edited by Lynn Z. Bloom, 8th ed., Houghton Mifflin, 2007, pp. 23–27.

Williams, Joseph. *Style: Ten Lessons in Clarity and Grace*. 7th ed., Addison-Wesley, 2003.

Winchester, Simon. *The Meaning of Everything: The Story of the Oxford English Dictionary*. Oxford UP, 2003.

Wolfram, Walt. "Linguistic and Sociolinguistic Requisites for Teaching Language." *Language Study in Middle School, High School, and Beyond: Views on Enhancing the Study of Language*, edited by John S. Simmons and Lawrence Baines, International Reading Association, 1998, pp. 79–109.

Young, Vershawn A., Rusty Barret, Y'Shanda Young-Rivera, and Kim B. Lovejoy. *Other People's English: Code-Meshing, Code-Switching, and African American Literacy*. Teachers College Press, 2014.

Literature Cited

Angelou, Maya. *I Know Why the Caged Bird Sings*. Bantam, 1969.

Austen, Jane. *Pride and Prejudice*. 1813. Viking, 2005.

Bedard, Michael. *Sitting Ducks*. Puffin, 1998.

Borden, Louise. *The Journey That Saved Curious George: The True Wartime Escape of Margret and H. A. Rey*. Illustrated by Allan Drummond, Houghton Mifflin, 2005.

Brontë, Emily. *Wuthering Heights*. 1847. TOR Books, 1988.

Brown, Margaret Wise. *The Important Book*. Illustrated by Leonard Weisgard, HarperCollins, 1949.

Burns, Olive Ann. *Cold Sassy Tree*. Dell, 1984.

Cather, Willa. *My Ántonia*. Houghton Mifflin, 1954.

Cazet, Denys. *The Perfect Pumpkin Pie*. Atheneum Books for Young Readers, 2005.

Charlip, Remy. *Fortunately*. Aladdin, 1964.

Choldenko, Gennifer. *Al Capone Does My Shirts*. Houghton Mifflin, 2004.

Cisneros, Sandra. *The House on Mango Street*. Vintage, 1984.

Crowe, Chris. *Mississippi Trial, 1955*. Phyllis Fogelman, 2002.

Dickens, Charles. *Great Expectations*. 1861. Signet, 1963.

———. *A Tale of Two Cities*. 1859. Signet, 1997.

Dillard, Annie. *An American Childhood*. Harper and Row, 1987.

Dunphy, Madeleine. *Here Is the African Savanna*. Illustrated by Tom Leonard, Web of Life Children's Books, 2006.

———. *Here Is the Tropical Rain Forest*. Illustrated by Michael Rothman, Web of Life Children's Books, 2006.

Fitzgerald, F. Scott. *The Great Gatsby*. Scribner, 1925.

Fritz, Jean. *Leonardo's Horse*. Illustrated by Hudson Talbott, G. P. Putnam's Sons, 2001.

Gall, Chris. *Dear Fish*. Little, Brown, 2006.

Golding, William. *Lord of the Flies*. Paragon Books, 1954.

Hawthorne, Nathaniel. *The Scarlet Letter*. 1850. Bantam, 1986.

Hesse, Karen. *Come On, Rain!* Scholastic, 1999.

Hurston, Zora Neale. *Their Eyes Were Watching God*. 1937. Perennial Classics, 1998.

Kingsolver, Barbara. *The Bean Trees*. HarperTorch, 1988.

Kingston, Maxine Hong. *The Woman Warrior: Memories of a Girlhood among Ghosts*. Vintage, 1989.

Knowles, John. *A Separate Peace*. Bantam, 1959.

Lee, Harper. *To Kill a Mockingbird*. Warner, 1960.

Marshall, James. *Swinelake*. Illustrated by Maurice Sendak, HarperCollins, 1999.

McDonald, Megan. *My House Has Stars*. Illustrated by Peter Catalanotto, Scholastic, 1996.

McKissack, Patricia C. *Flossie and the Fox*. Illustrated by Rachel Isadora, Dial Books for Young Readers, 1986.

Miller, Arthur. *The Crucible*. 1953. Penguin, 1976.

Monceaux, Morgan. *Jazz: My Music, My People*. Knopf, 1994.

Moore, Clement Clark. *'Twas the Night before Christmas, or Account of a Visit from St. Nicholas.* 1837. Candlewick, 2002.

Moss, Thylias. *I Want to Be.* Illustrated by Jerry Pinkney, Dial Books for Young Readers, 1993.

Myers, Walter Dean. *Monster.* Illustrated by Christopher Myers, Amistad, 1999.

Park, Linda S., and Julia Durango. *Yum! Yuck!* Illustrated by Sue Ramá, Charlesbridge, 2005.

Peck, Robert N. *A Day No Pigs Would Die.* Random House, 1972.

Philbrick, Rodman. *Freak the Mighty.* Scholastic, 2001.

Pinkney, Andrea Davis. *Duke Ellington.* Illustrated by Brian Pinkney, Hyperion, 1998.

Prelutsky, Jack. *If Not for the Cat.* Illustrated by Ted Rand, Greenwillow, 2004.

Rawls, Wilson. *Where the Red Fern Grows.* Bantam, 1961.

Robinson, Marc. *Cock-a-Doodle Doo! What Does It Sound Like to You?* Illustrated by Steve Jenkins, Stewart, Tabori, and Chang, 1993.

Rylant, Cynthia. *Long Night Moon.* Illustrated by Mark Siegel, Simon and Schuster, 2004.

———. *Scarecrow.* Illustrated by Lauren Stringer, Voyager, 1998.

Sendak, Maurice. *Where the Wild Things Are.* 1963. HarperCollins, 1991.

Shakespeare, William. *Romeo and Juliet.* 1597. Scholastic, 1969.

Steinbeck, John. *The Grapes of Wrath.* 1939. Penguin, 2002.

———. *Of Mice and Men.* 1937. Penguin, 1993.

———. *The Pearl.* 1947. Penguin, 2000.

Stoker, Bram. *Dracula.* 1897. Tom Doherty Associates, 1988.

Sweet, Melissa. *Some Writer! The Story of E. B. White.* Afterword by Martha White, Houghton Mifflin Harcourt, 2016.

Swift, Jonathan. "A Modest Proposal." *Literature: World Masterpieces,* edited by Roger Babusci et al., annotated teacher's ed., 4th ed., Prentice Hall, 1996, pp. 801–9.

Taback, Simms. *Kibitzers and Fools: Tales My Zayda Told Me.* Penguin, 2005.

Taylor, Mildred D. *The Land.* Penguin, 2003.

———. *Roll of Thunder, Hear My Cry.* Scholastic, 1976.

Thoreau, Henry David. *Walden and Civil Disobedience.* 1849, 1854. New American Library, 1980.

Tunnell, Michael O. *Halloween Pie.* Illustrated by Kevin O'Malley, Lothrop, Lee and Shepard, 1999.

Twain, Mark. *Adventures of Huckleberry Finn.* 1885. U of California P, 1988.

Tyson, Leigh Ann. *An Interview with Harry the Tarantula.* Illustrated by Henrik Drescher, National Geographic Society, 2003.

White, E. B. *The Trumpet of the Swan*. Scholastic, 1970.

———. *Stuart Little*. Harper and Brothers, 1945.

Wiesel, Elie. *Night*. 1960. Hill and Wang, 2006.

Williams, Carol Lynch. *My Angelica*. Random House, 1999.

Williams-Garcia, Rita. *One Crazy Summer*. Amistad, 2010.

Wisniewski, David. *The Secret Knowledge of Grown-Ups*. HarperTrophy, 1998.

Woodson, Jacqueline. *Show Way*. Putnam, 2005.

Young, Judy. *R Is for Rhyme: A Poetry Alphabet*. Illustrated by Victor Juhasz, Sleeping Bear Press, 2005.

Index

Note: A *t* following a page number indicates a table; an *f* indicates a figure.

Academic English, 100, 119–20. *See also* Standard English
Adjectives, 57–58, 69, 101–2, 109–10
Advertisements, 23, 46–48
Al Capone Does My Shirts (Choldenko), 60, 141, 142*t*
Alvarez, Julia, 23
An American Childhood (Dillard), 85
Analogy, 112–14
Anaphora, 91–92
Anderson, Jeff, 53
Andrews, Larry, 94
Animal sounds, 122
Appositives, 8, 124, 126–30
Assessments, 144, 145*f*
Atwell, Nancie, 13–14, 21–22
Audience, 41–43, 46–48, 114–16

Barret, Rusty, 18, 42, 43
Barry, Dave, 44, 137
Battistella, Edwin, 2, 43
The Bean Trees (Kingsolver), 77
Bedard, Michael, 40
Benjamin, Amy, 60, 66–67
Berger, Joan, 133
Birch, Barbara, 15, 17
Bomer, Randy, 38–39, 76
Borsheim-Black, Carlin, 78
Braddock, Richard, 2
Bresler, Ken, 91
Bryson, Bill, 21, 22

Burke, Jim
  definition of grammar, 6
  on ESL students, 107
  on grammar as process, 116
  on impact of grammar, 28, 29
  on learning grammar terminology, 110
  on rewriting, 37–38

Calvin and Hobbes cartoons, 20, 21*f*, 81*f*
Canby, Henry, 20
Carroll, Pamela Sissi, 119
Character development, 76–77
Chiu, Annette, 97
Christy, Janice, 96
Cinquain poems, 34–35
Class discussions, 145–47
Classroom activities
  adjectives, 109–10
  advertisements, 46–48
  appositives, 126–30
  collaborative writing, 107–8
  dialogue, 48–51
  grammar rant analysis, 43–44
  jazz rhythms, 51–52
  language formality/informality, 76–77
  language history lesson, 21–22
  letters for different audiences, 41–43
  metaphors, 117–18
  names and identity, 80
  participles and participial phrases, 66–69
  picture books, 45–46
  playful, 136–39
  poetry, 34–36

for punctuation, 38–41, 70–74
regionalisms, 121–22
rewriting from different perspectives, 36–38
sample lessons, 140–41*t*
scent memories, 57–58
sensitive language, 79
sentence combining, 53–56
sentence imitation, 56–58
Shakespearean language, 81–82
style shifting, 113–14
tone, 86–92
Worst Picture Book Ever, 104
Clauses, 156–57
Code-meshing, 18–19
Code-switching, 18
Collins, Valerie, 137, 138
Commas, 40–41, 111–12
Conjunctions, 66
Connors, Robert J., 137
Corbett, Edward P. J., 137
Criminal justice system, 24
Critical thinking, 23–24, 44
Crovitz, Darren, 5, 6, 24, 90, 100
Crowe, Chris, 50
Cruz, Mary C., 120
Crystal, David, 23
Curzan, Anne, 22, 138

Dashes, 74
Dean, Deborah, 4, 53
Dear Fish (Gall), 65–66
Declarative sentences, 86–89
Denham, Kristin, 20
Dependent clauses, 125
Description, 66–69
Devereaux, Michelle, 5, 6, 24, 90, 100
Dialects. *See also* Standard English
   academic English, 100
   and character development, 76–77
   and emotion, 74–76
   formal/informal speech, 76–77, 112–14
   regionalisms, 121–22
   students' awareness of, 16–17
Dialogue, 48–51, 64
Diamante poems, 35–36

Didion, Joan, 53
Di Gennaro, Kristen, 113
Dong, Yu Ren, 116–17, 118
Doniger, Paul, 59
Donna, Jeannine M., 7
Doublets, 36
Duke Ellington (Pinkney), 51–52
Dunn, Patricia A., 42, 43–44

Eats, Shoots and Leaves: The Zero Tolerance Approach to Punctuation (Truss), 70
Eats, Shoots and Leaves: Why, Commas Really Do Make a Difference! (Truss), 139
Editing, 11–14, 38–39, 110–12. *See also* Punctuation
Ehrenworth, Mary
   on goal of grammar instruction, 7
   on grammar and writing, 28–29
   on grammar rules, 13–14
   on mentor texts, 38
   on power dynamics, 15
ELLs
   and academic writing, 119
   demographics of, 94
   grammar correction as ineffective for, 99
   and idioms, 96–97
   and literature, 97–98
   and mentor texts, 98
   and metaphors, 117
   necessary information for teachers of, 95–96
   and reading aloud, 97–98
   and test preparation, 106–7
Emotion, 74–76, 83–85
English language learners (ELLs). *See* ELLs
Epistrophe, 92
Exclamatory sentences, 86–89

Flossie and the Fox (McKissack), 77
Formal speech, 76–77, 112–14
Fortunately (Charlip), 107–8
Fragments. *See* Sentence fragments
Francis, W. Nelson, 5
Fravel, L. A., 45

Lindblom, Kenneth, 42, 43–44
Literature, 97–98
Long Night Moon (Rylant), 111
Lord of the Flies (Golding), 69
Lyiscott, Jamila, 16

Massey, Lance, 71
McWhorter, John, 20
Meaning
    grammar's role in creating, 60, 71
    and language change, 24
    and punctuation, 12–13, 38–39, 41,
        70–74
    and rhetorical choices, 83–85
    and sentence structures, 51–53
Memes, 136–37
Mentor texts
    and ELLs, 98
    for punctuation, 40–41
    and rhetorical grammar, 25
    and sentence combining, 25–26
    and sentence imitation, 25–26, 56–58
    and verb tenses, 38
Metaphors, 116–19
Meyer, Jim, 103
Micciche, Laura, 53
Minor sentences. *See* Sentence fragments
Mississippi Trial, 1955 (Crowe), 57, 69
Mitchell, Koritha, 78
"A Modest Proposal" (Swift), 71–73
Murfin, Ross, 117
My Angelica (Williams), 118
My Ántonia (Cather), 70
Myers, Marshall, 90
Myhill, Debra, 3, 33–34, 103
My House Has Stars (McDonald), 98

Names and naming, 79–80
Napoli, Donna J., 48, 49, 50
National Council of Teachers of English
    (NCTE). *See* NCTE/IRA Standards
NCTE/IRA Standards, 8, 60
"NCTE Position Paper on the Role of
    English Teachers in Educating English
    Language Learners (ELLs)," 96, 98, 99
Night (Wiesel), 83–85
Nilsen, 117

Noden, Harry
    on participial phrases, 65, 68
    on punctuation, 38, 61
    on terminology, 8, 10
    on value of teaching grammar, 7
Noguchi, Rei R., 11
Nouns, 155
Nunan, Susan, 146
"N-word," 78–79

One Crazy Summer (Williams-Garcia),
    101–2, 116, 130

Paragrams, 137–38
Paragraphs, 84
Parallelism, 91
Paraskevas, Cornelia, 123
Parkes, Malcolm B., 12
Participial phrases, 35, 65, 68, 124
Participles, 8, 65, 67–69
Parts of speech, 155–56
Pauses, 70–71
The Pearl (Steinbeck), 55–56
Penha, James, 7
The Perfect Pumpkin Pie (Cazet), 76–77
Perin, Dolores, 34, 53
Perrin, Robert, 48
Persuasion, 46–48
Petit, Angela, 72
Phrases, 156
Picture books
    *Cock-a-Doodle Doo! What Does It Sounds
        Like to You?* (Robinson), 122
    Dear Fish (Gall), 65–66
    *Eats, Shoots and Leaves: The Zero Toler-
        ance Approach to Punctuation* (Truss),
        139
    *Eats, Shoots and Leaves: Why, Commas
        Really Do Make a Difference!* (Truss),
        139
    Flossie and the Fox (McKissack), 77
    Halloween Pie (Tunnell), 64–65
    Kibitzers and Fools (Taback), 49
    The Perfect Pumpkin Pie (Cazet), 76–77
    reading aloud, 97
    Where the Wild Things Are (Sendak),
        109

wordless, 45–46, 45*f*
Worst Picture Book Ever, 104
Yum! Yuck! (Park and Durango), 122
Poetry
    and grammar instruction, 34–36
    punctuation as meaningful in, 71
Politeness, 114–15
Political speeches, 23–24
Pollio, Howard R., 117
Postman, Neil, 7
Poth, Joseph, 106
Power dynamics, 14–19, 24, 44
Pragmatics, 114–16
Prepositions, 155
Pugh, Sharon, 116, 118
Punctuation. *See also* specific items
    appositives, 129
    and dialogue, 50
    editing for, 11–14
    as guideline vs. rule, 38–39, 61
    history of, 11–12
    and meaning, 12–13, 38–39, 41, 70–74
    and mentor texts, 40–41
    mini-lessons, 13–14
    reading aloud, 14
    and tone, 88
    "Victor Borge" method, 110–11
Puns, 137–38

Racial slurs, 78–79
Rap poetry, 36
Raub, Albert, 1
Ray, Supriya, 117
Reading aloud
    and ELLs, 97–98
    for punctuation learning, 14
    and sentence structures, 51–52
Reading comprehension, 59–63
ReadWriteThink.org, 113, 139, 140–41*t*
Regionalisms, 121–22
Repetition, 90–92
Rhetorical grammar
    definition of, 25
    and mentor texts, 25–26
    structure and meaning, 83–85
    and stylistic devices, 26–27

Roberts, Doralyn R., 146
Romano, Tom, 39, 105
Romeo and Juliet (Shakespeare), 79, 81–82

Sanders, Ella, 21
Sarigianides, Sophia, 78
Satire, 137
Scarecrow (Rylant), 56, 91–92
Schultz, Irene, 113
Schuster, Edgar H.
    on dialects, 16
    on learning grammar terminology, 11, 103
    on mentor texts, 25
    on paragraphs, 84
    on punctuation, 12
    on sentence fragments, 89
    on traditional grammar instruction, 9
Schwartz, Adam, 38
Semicolons, 72–73
Sentence fragments, 31–33, 52, 62–63, 89
Sentences
    combining, 25–26, 53–56, 126–30
    functions of, 86
    imitating, 25–26, 54, 56–58, 123–26
    type of, and tone, 86–90
Sentence structures
    and meaning, 51–53
    overview of, 157–58
    and reading aloud, 51–52
Shafer, Gregory, 41–43
Shakespeare, William, 80–82
Show Way (Woodson), 76
Similes, 117, 118
Simmons, Eileen, 59
Smith, Michael W., 9–10
Smoot, Scott W., 105, 106
Sorensen, S., 133
Spelling, 22–23
Standard English. *See also* Usage
    and academic writing, 100, 119–20
    definition of, 15
    as "high style," 76
    limitations of, 74
    power dynamics of, 14–19
Standardized tests. *See* Tests

Author

Deborah Dean is fascinated with language. She regu-
larly brings humor to others' lives by commenting on
some felicity of language that catches her fancy: they
laugh, roll their eyes, and move on. But that doesn't
stop her from noticing and thinking about the whys
and the hows of language as it is used by the world
around her. She used to teach junior high and high
school students about language, hoping to ignite
within them the curiosity about language she thinks
it deserves—after all, we are surrounded by language
in a variety of forms every waking minute. Now she teaches preservice teachers
and tries to do the same thing—help them develop their interest and curiosity
about language and how it works. Deborah is the author of numerous articles,
some quick-reference guides, and several books, including *Strategic Writing* (2nd
ed.), *Genre Theory*, and *What Works in Writing Instruction* (2nd ed.), and, with Jeff
Anderson, *Revision Decisions*. When she's not writing or teaching, she likes to
bake cookies and spend time with her family.

This book was typeset in TheMix and Palatino by Barbara Frazier.

Typefaces used on the cover include Gotham Book and Lu Px.

The book was printed on 50-lb. White Offset paper by Seaway Printing Company, Inc.